Pioneers Of Forest And City

JAMES J. BLANCHARD
GOVERNOR

September 1, 1985

Michigan has a rich and proud history. From our early times of Indians living in kinship with nature to our more recent history of tremendous scientific and technological change, the people of Michigan have shown great strength in meeting new challenges.

Knowing what happened in the past provides us with valuable information to help us prepare for the future. This book is more than just a history lesson; it is a legacy of courage, faith and inspiration upon which we can build.

We are still learning from the deeds of those who came before us. Their willingness to learn new skills and their energy to tackle new challenges hold valuable lessons for us today.

As you read through these pages, try to look beyond the historical events and people, and think of them as building blocks for our future. If we use these lessons, we can make Michigan's future even greater than our glorious past.

James J. Blanchard
Governor

Pioneers of Forest and City

by Harry Stapler
with Berenice Lowe and
Amy South

Lansing
Michigan Historical Commission
Bureau of History
Michigan Department of State
1985

Library of Congress Catalog Number 85-062817

 1

TABLE OF CONTENTS

FOREWORD

Pioneers of Forest and City is the last in a group of books funded by a bequest from Dr. John M. Munson. Born in Pennsylvania in 1878, Dr. Munson moved to Menominee County, Michigan, in 1890. His lifelong devotion to education culminated in the presidency of Michigan State Normal College (now Eastern Michigan University) from 1933 to 1948. He died in 1950. Because Dr. Munson "considered it important that the citizens of Michigan have adequate and correct knowledge of the history and functions of the state of Michigan and its institutions," he directed that the Michigan Historical Commission use funds from his estate to provide a textbook on the history of Michigan plus a history of education in Michigan. The first of these, *Michigan in Four Centuries*, a high-school text by F. Clever Bald, was published in 1954. This was followed by a four-volume history of education in Michigan, as well as a variety of pamphlets and booklets that are used by educators throughout the state. The Michigan Historical Commission, which has administered the Munson bequest, believed that in order to carry out the intent as well as the exact wording of Dr. Munson's will, an elementary Michigan history text should also be published. Thus, this history of Michigan for young people completes the commission's program for carrying out Dr. Munson's intent and, with the other volumes, composes the John M. Munson legacy.

By happy coincidence, *Pioneers of Forest and City* is being published as Michigan begins its celebration of 150 years of statehood, and the Michigan Sesquicentennial Commission has adopted this book as a Michigan Sesquicentennial Publication. It is our hope that the celebration of the sesquicentennial will serve to reinforce the educational aims that John M. Munson had in mind when he directed the Michigan Historical Commission to publish "a history suitable for the elementary and high schools."

Richard H. Austin
Secretary of State
Lansing, August 30, 1985

John Swainson, President
Michigan Historical Commission
Manchester, August 30, 1985

ACKNOWLEDGMENTS

Pioneers of Forest and City is the product of many hands working over many years. Berenice Lowe of Battle Creek drafted the first text and then worked with Amy South of the same city to develop the original plan for the book. Janet E. Alleman of Michigan State University edited that text with an eye to a vocabulary suitable for young people. After the Bureau of History decided to alter the text to include more material on twentieth-century Michigan, Harry Stapler, a professor of journalism (then at Michigan State University and now at the University of Florida) rewrote the text. Sandra S. Clark and Dr. Roger L. Rosentreter of the Bureau of History edited and produced the book.

The design of the book, too, must be credited to several people. Susan Price of Ann Arbor created the overall design and provided illustrations and page design for much of the book. Kelly Nelson, also of Ann Arbor, provided other illustrations, including that used on the cover. Dottie-Kay Bowersox of Duet Graphics in Jackson completed the design of the book.

Many other people helped along the way by reviewing the text and offering advice. We are grateful to all of them!

Dr. Martha M. Bigelow
Director, Bureau of History
Michigan Department of State
Lansing
September 1, 1985

PREFACE

In this book, you will read stories about success and failure, about happiness and sadness, about progress and frustration, about agreement and conflict.

In the grand sweep of Michigan's history, in our state's forests and its cities, you will see how things change and develop. You will see how men and women influence change. Change requires work and takes time. Sometimes the results of hard work do not show immediately. Many things that will happen during your life are just beginning to take shape now.

It helps us to know what happened in the past. That knowledge can help us handle challenges and improve our lives. If we do not know history, we are likely to repeat our mistakes. If we know history, we are likely to make better decisions.

You might compare a good student of history with a good sailor. With a sense of history, you have a good compass to direct you and a strong, fresh wind for sailing. You can put up more sail and sail farther. You can survive more storms. You can sail into more ports. Happy sailing!

Harry Stapler
Gainesville, Florida
September 1, 1985

The map shows labels: Menominee, Chippewa (Ojibwa), Ottawa, Potawatomi, Wyandot (Huron), Miami.

THE FIRST STORY

In this chapter Indians are the only people living in what will become Michigan. These Indians do not write, but they leave behind objects called artifacts that will help us imagine what their lives were like. Some of the Indians hunt and fish. Others also grow food. Some do a lot of trading.

PEOPLE

Makons (may-cons), an imaginary boy, was a member of the Chippewa tribe.

Medweackwe (mad-way-ak-way) was Makons' sister.

The **Chippewa** were also called the **Ojibwa.** Around 1600, many lived in what is now the Upper Peninsula. They fished and hunted for most of their food.

The **Menominee** lived in the southwest part of the Upper Peninsula.

The **Ottawa** lived in the northern part of the Lower Peninsula and were great traders.

The **Potawatomi** and **Miami** lived in southwest Michigan.

The **Wyandot** or **Huron** lived in southeast Michigan and grew much of their food.

2

WORDS

Prehistoric people lived before people wrote and read about the story of their past, which is called their history.

An **archaeologist** studies objects that reveal how people used to live.

An **artifact** is something people make. An arrowhead is an Indian artifact. A pencil is a modern artifact.

A **wigwam** is a round, dome-shaped home made by stretching animal skins and tree bark over poles. Most Michigan Indians lived in wigwams.

A **long house** is a large bark-covered building that many families live in. The Huron were the only Michigan Indians who lived in long houses.

WHEN DID IT HAPPEN?

	I About 9000 BC:	The earliest people we know about live in the Detroit area									
		About 100 BC:	People in Michigan begin to grow food in gardens						I		
			About AD 1600:	The Indians described in this chapter live in what is now Michigan						I	
	Around 1620:	The first European, or white man, comes to Michigan								I	
					You and your parents					▷	
10000 BC	8000 BC	6000 BC	4000 BC	2000 BC	0	AD 2000					

Kelly Nelson

CHAPTER ONE
MICHIGAN'S FIRST PEOPLE

The Indian boy, tall and strong, was 13 years old. He lived with his family beside a river about 400 years ago. They lived in what is now known as the Upper Peninsula. Giant trees rose above the village's wigwams. In those years before the white man came, great forests covered nearly all of what we now call Michigan.

The boy was a Chippewa. His name was Makons (may-cons). That meant Little Bear. Makons had three older brothers and a younger sister. His brothers were adults.

They hunted and fished with the men of the village. Makons and his sister were still children. They helped their parents work, but they also had time to play.

Makons and his sister did not go to school. But they had to learn how to find and cook food, make clothes and build homes. They had to learn the rules about living with the other people in their tribe. They learned by watching older people work, by helping do the work, and by listening to the stories their parents and other older people told about the past.

Summer had nearly ended. It was what the Indians called the "Turning of the Leaves Moon." For Makons this was an important time. One day his parents told him he was old enough to go to the woods to try to find his special spirit. Every Chippewa young person made this trip alone. They took no food or water with them.

The next day Makons put on his deerskin shirt, his leggings and his moccasins. He left his family and walked on a narrow trail along a ridge into the woods. After a while, he found a place to stay and made a bed using pine branches.

It grew dark. Makons was alone and hungry. Leaves rustled above him. Some wolves howled. He prayed to the spirits to pity him and send him a vision or dream. The spirit that visited him during this dream would help him the rest of his life.

Indians believed that each thing around them had a spirit. Some spirits were kind. Some were mean. When a Chippewa hunter killed an animal for food, he offered a sacrifice to its spirit and thanked it for giving him food.

Makons knew that if he dreamed about a spirit, he could go home happy. He also knew he might spend more than one night in the woods waiting for such a dream to visit him.

At last, on the third night, Makons dreamed about a moose running along a forest path. When he woke up, Makons knew his own spirit and the moose's spirit had united. He hurried back to his wigwam. Joyfully he told his family about his dream. His family gave him a special adult name, Running Moose.

Indians often had more than one name. Some names came from things they did. Sometimes a medicine man gave a powerful name to a sick person to help that person get well.

A year later, when the Turning of the Leaves Moon came again, Makons' sister went to seek a vision or dream. Her name

Archaeologists must carefully remove layers of dirt to expose artifacts used by earlier civilizations. They use hand tools and work slowly to discover the relationships between artifacts.

was Medweackwe (mad-way-ak-way), Noise of the Wind in the Trees. An old man gave her this name because she cried a lot when she was a baby.

Medweackwe too went into the woods. On her first night she dreamed about beautiful red flowers. They became her spirit.

THE PREHISTORIC INDIANS

Before the white man came, Indians lived in the land now known as Michigan for about ten thousand years. They did not write books or keep records, so it is not easy to learn about their lives.

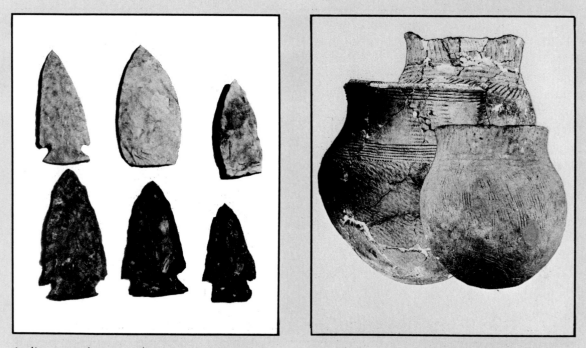

Indians used projectile points or arrowheads chipped from stone (above left) for arrows and spears. These 1,000-year-old clay pots (above right) are from southern Michigan.

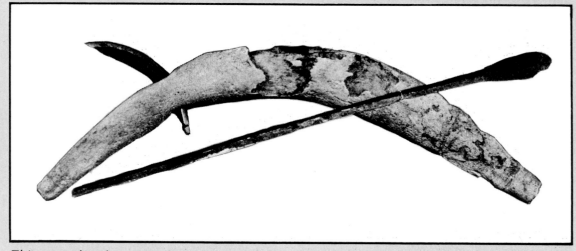

This curved antler with a beaver tooth mounted in it was probably used as a digging tool by Michigan Indians over 500 years before the arrival of whites in Michigan. The straight copper awl shown with it was used to punch holes in such things as leather.

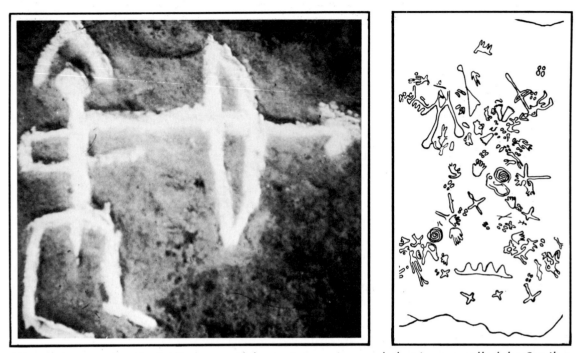

We are not certain why Indians carved these pictures in a rock that is now called the Sanilac Petroglyphs in Sanilac County. But the carvings may have been part of a religion practiced by people as long as a thousand years ago.

The clues to how they lived come from their village sites and graves. There archaeologists have found objects or artifacts that once belonged to the Indians.

The first Michigan people archaeologists know about lived around 11,000 years ago. They hunted wild animals and traveled in small groups.

As the centuries passed, some prehistoric Indians learned how to make clay pots and copper beads and tools. They made tools and weapons from bone antlers and flint. They traded with other Indians.

About 2,000 years ago, some Indians began planting crops. They did not move as often as had their ancestors, and they lived in larger groups. By the time the first white man came to Michigan around 1620, these groups were organized tribes.

MICHIGAN'S SIX INDIAN TRIBES

When Europeans found Michigan in 1620, parts of six tribes spent most of their time here. They were the Chippewa, the Ottawa, the Potawatomi, the Miami, the Menominee and the Wyandot. Other tribes sometimes traveled through Michigan.

Five of the six tribes in Michigan in 1620 spoke languages that were alike. They were called the Algonquian languages. These

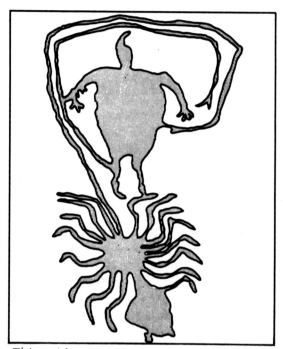

This spiderman is an Indian pictograph or rock carving from Burnt Bluff on the Garden Peninsula in Delta County.

were the Chippewa (or Ojibwa), Ottawa, Potawatomi, Miami and Menominee tribes.

The Wyandot tribe was different. It was related to the Iroquois, most of whom lived east of Michigan. The Wyandot spoke an Iroquoian language. The Wyandot sometimes were called the Huron. They lived in the Detroit area and grew crops for food. Their villages did not move from place to place as often as Algonquian villages did.

The various small Indian villages of the five Algonquian tribes rarely stayed in any one place long. When food and supplies ran out, and as the seasons changed, the village moved. There was much land, and

there were only about 15,000 Indians in Michigan in 1620.

The Chippewa, the tribe of Makons and Medweackwe, lived throughout the Upper Peninsula. The Menominee lived in the southwest part of the Upper Peninsula.

In the northern Lower Peninsula were the Ottawa. Some Potawatomi were in the western Lower Peninsula. A few Miami lived in southwest Michigan.

INDIAN BELIEFS

Each Indian tribe had its own ways and beliefs, but the tribes shared three beliefs:
1. The Indians believed in special spirits, or gods. Spirits were more powerful than men. They could help or hurt men.
2. The Indians believed in sharing. They knew they had to work together to survive. They also believed that nature—the land, animals and plants—belonged to everyone.
3. The Indians believed in individual freedom. No one had the right to run another's life. A group followed a chief only if it believed he was a good leader. This meant Michigan Indians seldom were organized into large groups. If someone did not like what his group was doing, he found a new group or moved to another village.

INDIAN TRANSPORTATION

Makons, Medweackwe and their friends traveled by foot and canoe. Michigan Indians used bark canoes. They built a frame of slender cedar logs. Elm or birch bark covered the frame. The Indians sewed the bark together with strong, soft roots of black spruce or cedar trees. To keep water out, they sealed the canoe with spruce or pine gum.

The canoe did many things well. Because it had a rounded, flat bottom, it floated high in the water. Therefore it could be used on shallow streams. It was light. An Indian could carry a canoe overland when he came to a waterfall or rapids.

When the Indians traveled by land they used trails. Sometimes so many people or animals had walked on a trail that it was easy to follow. Sometimes landmarks, such as streams or crooked trees, were used to tell where a trail was. The trails in the forest usually were narrow, just wide enough for one person's body. One of the things Makons had to learn was how to find and follow the trails that his tribe used.

INDIAN WORK

To people who live in houses and ride in cars, the way the Indians lived seems very hard. They had to hunt or grow their own food. They made their own weapons, tools, homes and clothes. Even with everyone working, a village might not have enough to eat if the winter was especially long and the hunting was not good.

But the Indians did not think this was a bad way to live. They were not always happy, but they found much to enjoy. They were close to their village friends and to nature. Their religious beliefs helped them understand their world.

When the Indians wanted or needed something they did not have, they traded with other Indians to get it. That is how Indians in Michigan got Atlantic Ocean sea-

shells to use as beads. Sometimes Indians traded things to show friendship. The Ottawa were especially good traders.

All members of a family worked. Makons, like other Chippewa men, made and repaired snowshoes, traps, wooden tools and canoes. The men hunted with bows and arrows, spears and traps. They were very good fishermen.

Medweackwe and her mother tanned (softened) the skins of the animals and made them into clothing. They wove fishnets and mats. They chopped wood. They cooked. They made the wooden buckets used for maple syrup. They cut and wove the bark coverings for their wigwam.

Indian parents were kind to their children. Indians did not spank children, but children who did not work got no supper. A child who misbehaved might be drenched in water. And children feared the spirits would punish them if they were very bad.

At night, families might sit around a fire. The children listened to older people tell stories of their ancestors, of kind and unkind spirits, and of the deeds of heroes. This was how Indian children learned about their history and about how they were expected to act as adults.

INDIAN DRESS

Michigan Indians did not wear feathered headdresses. Much of the time they went bareheaded. They wore their hair long and kept it smooth by rubbing bear grease into it. Sometimes they braided their hair. Some men shaved their heads. They left a strip of hair only in the middle. Some men decorated their hair with beads.

This painting shows how Michigan Indians lived before the arrival of the white man. The Indians used the bark from birch trees for their wigwams (center) and for canoes (right).

Women did most of the chores in prehistoric Indian villages. Besides making maple sugar (above), the women also planted and harvested all of the crops.

Indian men did all the hunting. Spearing fish (left) was another form of obtaining food. Building the birchbark wigwam (right) was a job for the women.

Women also braided their hair. They sometimes fastened otter fur to their braids.

During cold weather, both men and women wore fur hats and leather moccasins, leggings and shirts. They often decorated their shirts. The women also wore knee-length deerskin skirts. In cold weather, Indians sometimes draped fur blankets over their shoulders.

In the summer, men like Makons wore only moccasins and a breech cloth.

INDIAN HOMES

Michigan's five Algonquian tribes lived in dome-shaped wigwams. For their wigwam, Makons and his brothers and father cut down saplings (young trees). They stripped off the branches. Then they peeled sheets of bark from some very large trees.

Medweackwe, her mother and aunts stuck the saplings in the ground in a circle. Then they bent the saplings and tied them together at the top using green basswood strips. Finally they covered the frame with the sheets of birch, cedar and elm bark.

The family dug a pit in the center of the wigwam for a fireplace. The fire would heat the wigwam and give light at night. They left a hole at the top for smoke to escape. When it rained they covered the hole. In cold weather, they placed an animal skin over the door. Cooking and eating was done outdoors unless the weather was bad.

When the family moved to a new place, they left the sapling framework behind. But they rolled up the bark covering and took it along. They would use it to cover their new wigwam.

At night, the Chippewa slept between animal skins. Feathers of wild ducks or many pieces of soft, dried plants were placed under the skins.

The Wyandots lived in long houses instead of wigwams. Sometimes the long houses were 100 feet long and 12 feet wide. Many families lived in a single long house. Like wigwams, long houses were built by covering a wooden framework with bark and furs. Inside, a middle passage ran from end to end and contained fire pits. Each family had its own area on one side of the passage.

INDIAN FOOD

Michigan Indians obtained food in many ways. From the woods and along the streams, they gathered berries, grapes, acorns, nuts and wild rice. They grew corn, beans and squash in gardens. From streams and lakes, they took fish. From the woods, they took animals. The Potawatomi and Wyandot Indians of southern Michigan farmed more than did the Indians of northern Michigan.

The Chippewa family of Makons and Medweackwe lived in the Upper Peninsula. In the spring, they collected sap from maple trees. From that they made maple syrup. The summer was the best time for fishing. They also did a little gardening. In late summer, they collected berries, wild rice and other wild foods. They would save some of these for winter.

In the fall, the men and older boys went hunting for bear, moose, deer, wolf and fox. They used bows and arrows, traps and snares. In the winter they continued to hunt and ate their stored food. If the hunting was bad, they might not have enough to eat.

INDIAN MEDICINE

Indians believed that medicine men could influence the spirit world. Lucky and unlucky spirits lived in the bodies of people and animals. They also were in all parts of nature. The Indians believed that medicine men, working with the spirits, could make sick people well. Sometimes the medicine worked. Sometimes it did not.

When Makons became ill one spring, a medicine man made some medicine from roots, seeds and barks. He covered Makons with the medicine. He hoped to sicken the evil spirit and force him to leave Makons' body. Eventually Makons got well.

When Makons' grandfather became ill, the medicine man tried to frighten the evil away. He beat drums and shook rattles. He danced and shouted wildly. But Makons' grandfather died. The medicine man's magic had not been strong enough.

An Ottawa Indian made this glove box from porcupine quills and birch bark in 1895. Ottawa Indians were doing quillwork as early as 1615 when the French first met them.

INDIAN WARFARE

Some Indians became chiefs mainly because they were leaders of war or raiding parties. No one, however, was forced to follow a chief into a battle. The braves went only if they trusted the chief.

Michigan's Indians were not as warlike as the fierce Iroquois, who lived east of Michigan. The Michigan Indians believed in individual choice, and it was hard to get large numbers of them to agree to fight.

When they fought, it was sometimes because another group moved too close to their territory. They also might fight to revenge a wrong done to one of them by someone from another village or tribe.

Raids often took place in the fall, after the winter supplies had been gathered. The men who agreed to go on the raid wore and carried as little as possible. They applied war paint in order to gain help from the spirit world and frighten the enemy. They traveled quickly and quietly in order to surprise the enemy. They fought only as long as they seemed to be winning. They thought it was foolish to continue to fight when one was losing. It was better to retreat and save the lives of men who could fight again later.

MICHIGAN'S INDIAN HERITAGE

Many Michigan rivers and places have Indian names. Michigan itself comes from an Indian language. "Michi" means great; "gane" means lake or water. The Indians used the word to describe Lake Michigan.

14

This box is made of birchbark sheets and porcupine quills that have been dyed.

Some Michigan counties that took the names of tribes are Chippewa, Ottawa, Huron and Menominee. Counties named after chiefs are Sanilac, Osceola and Newaygo. Some counties have geographical meanings. Saginaw means mouth of the river. Muskegon means marshy river. Lenawee means man. And Washtenaw means hinterlands.

The Indians gave Michigan more than names. They taught Michigan's first white people how to live in the wilderness—to make canoes and maple sugar, and to hunt. They hunted for the furs that brought the first white people to Michigan.

The Indians also knew something it took the white man a long time to learn. The Indians knew that they had to respect and live in harmony with the land and nature. They could not live without forests, clear streams and lakes, fish and animals. It is only in recent years that Michigan's other settlers have realized that these natural resources must be taken care of if we do not want to lose them.

CONCLUSION

Indians have lived in Michigan for at least 11,000 years. We do not know a lot about the early Indians, but we can imagine how Indians like Makons and Medweackwe lived just before the first white man came to Michigan around 1620.

Indians in Michigan in 1620 belonged to the Chippewa, Menominee, Ottawa, Potawatomi, Miami and Wyandot tribes.

Each tribe had its own special ways of living and doing things. Michigan's Indians traveled by canoe or on foot. They did not make war as often as did some North American Indians.

The Wyandot were an Iroquoian tribe. They lived in long houses, farmed and did not move often. The others were Algonquian tribes. They lived in wigwams and moved often to find better places to fish, hunt and gather food.

All Michigan's Indians had religious beliefs about the spirit world. They shared their food and possessions with other people in their villages. They believed people should be independent and think for themselves. They thought the land and nature belonged to everyone.

In the next chapter we will find out what happened when the French joined the Indians in Michigan.

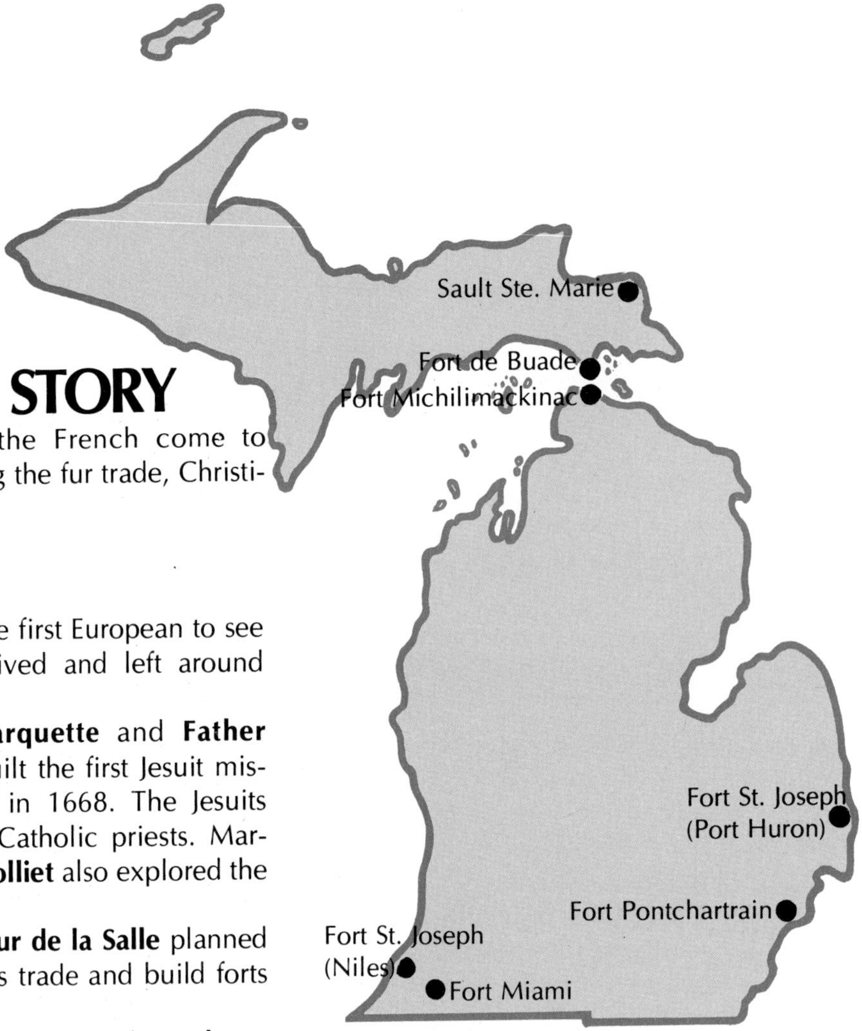

THE NEXT STORY

In this chapter, the French come to Michigan. They bring the fur trade, Christianity and settlers.

PEOPLE

Etienne Brulé was the first European to see Michigan. He arrived and left around 1620.

Father Jacques Marquette and **Father Claude Dablon** built the first Jesuit mission in Michigan in 1668. The Jesuits were a group of Catholic priests. Marquette and **Louis Jolliet** also explored the Mississippi River.

Robert Cavelier, Sieur de la Salle planned to expand France's trade and build forts in the West.

Marie-Thérèse Cadillac and **Madame Tonty,** the first white women to live in Michigan, arrived in 1701. Their husbands commanded the new fort at Detroit.

PLACES

Fort Miami was built in 1679 by La Salle near the present city of St. Joseph.

Fort St. Joseph (Port Huron) was located on Lake Huron. The French occupied it for only two years, from 1686 to 1688.

Fort de Buade was built in 1690 at St. Ignace.

Fort St. Joseph (Niles) had the same name as the fort at Port Huron. Built in 1691, it stood on the main trade and war routes in southwestern Michigan.

Fort Pontchartrain was built by Cadillac in 1701 at Detroit.

Fort Michilimackinac was built around 1715 to protect the Straits of Mackinac.

Sault Ste. Marie was Michigan's first missionary and trading outpost.

Sault Ste. Marie

Fort de Buade
Fort Michilimackinac

Fort St. Joseph (Port Huron)

Fort Pontchartrain

Fort St. Joseph (Niles)

Fort Miami

WORDS

Coureurs du bois were independent French fur traders.

Voyageurs were hired by merchant firms to transport trade goods and furs by canoe.

New France was the name of the French colonies in North America.

Fasting means to go without eating for a long time.

WHEN DID IT HAPPEN

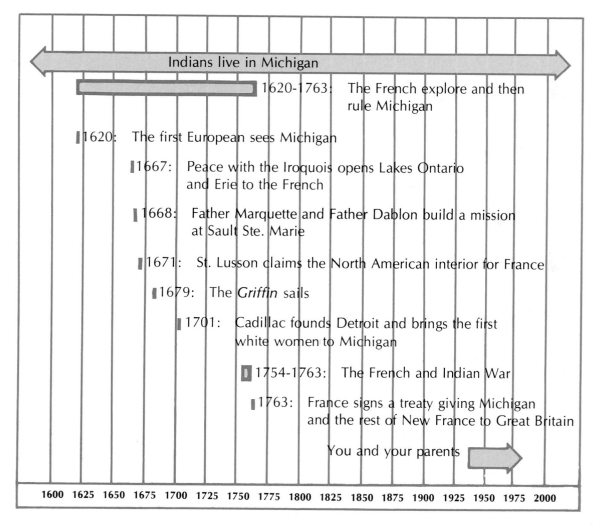

Indians live in Michigan

1620-1763: The French explore and then rule Michigan

1620: The first European sees Michigan

1667: Peace with the Iroquois opens Lakes Ontario and Erie to the French

1668: Father Marquette and Father Dablon build a mission at Sault Ste. Marie

1671: St. Lusson claims the North American interior for France

1679: The *Griffin* sails

1701: Cadillac founds Detroit and brings the first white women to Michigan

1754-1763: The French and Indian War

1763: France signs a treaty giving Michigan and the rest of New France to Great Britain

You and your parents

1600 1625 1650 1675 1700 1725 1750 1775 1800 1825 1850 1875 1900 1925 1950 1975 2000

17

CHAPTER TWO
THE FRENCH
JOIN THE INDIANS

The year was 1701. No longer were Indians the only people in Michigan's forests. A few hundred white explorers, missionaries and fur traders from France were there, too. They were all men. There were no white women in Michigan.

A small band of Iroquois Indians was camped on the shore of Lake Erie, near the mouth of the Detroit River. One morning, these Indians saw a strange sight—two white women riding in canoes. White men were paddling the canoes. The Indians had never seen a white woman that far west.

The white women were Madame Cadillac and Madame Tonty. They would soon be the first white women to see what is now Michigan. With them was Madame Cadillac's youngest son, Jacques.

Madame Cadillac and Madame Tonty were on their way to join their husbands at Fort Pontchartrain. The fort had just been built where Detroit now stands. The commander of the new fort was Antoine de la Mothe Cadillac. Second in command was Alphonse de Tonty.

Cadillac had convinced the king of France that this was the best place in the Great Lakes for a large, important fort. People from England, Spain and Holland also lived in North America. The French wanted to be sure these other people did not get the land around the Great Lakes. Cadillac thought a fort at Detroit would give France control of the Indians, the furs and the land around the Great Lakes.

SusanPrice

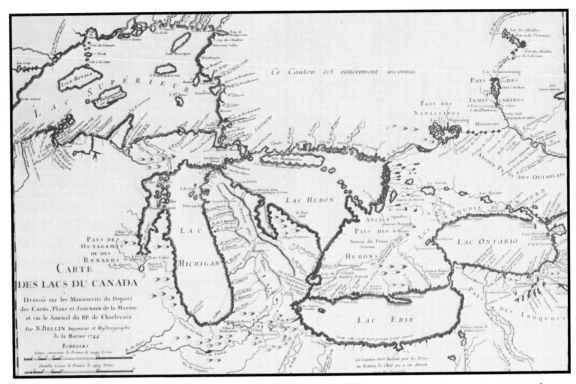

Early maps of the Great Lakes had many mistakes. This map was drawn in 1744 by a Frenchman. Michigan and the Great Lakes have strange shapes, and there are several large islands in Lake Superior that do not really exist.

Other people thought the French should stay at Quebec and Montreal. It was easier to protect these places. They wanted Cadillac to fail. They said things like: "The new fort is only a temporary fort. It is not a good place to settle. Cadillac won't stay." Cadillac needed to show people that he would stay.

He asked his wife, Marie-Thérèse, to come from Quebec and live with him. Back in Quebec, her friends told her not to go. They said the fort was too far away and too dangerous.

Marie-Thérèse looked her friends in the face and said: "Do not waste your pity on me, dear friends. I know the hardships, the perils of the journey, the isolation of the life to which I am going. Yet I am eager to go. For a woman who loves her husband has no stronger attachment than his company, wherever that may be."

So she and Madame Tonty went to Detroit. When the women arrived at the fort, they were greeted by Cadillac and Tonty, French soldiers, priests, fur traders and Indians. They all held a party by the river.

20

EUROPEANS COME TO AMERICA

In the seventeenth century, people from four European nations explored and settled North America.

People from France chose the continent's most northern part, including Canada, the Great Lakes and Michigan.

Those from Spain went to the warmer, southern regions, including Florida and the Gulf of Mexico.

Most Englishmen stayed along the East Coast, from Massachusetts in the north to Georgia in the south. Some also went to Hudson Bay in the far north.

People from the Netherlands lived along the Hudson River in what is now New York.

All traded with the Indians, and all wanted more land. Some were enemies in Europe. When nations fought each other in Europe, their colonies sometimes fought in North America too. Britain and France did most of the fighting in North America.

THE FIRST FRENCHMAN IN MICHIGAN

The first Europeans in North America were seeking a direct water passage to the Pacific Ocean and China. They wanted to trade more easily for Chinese silks and spices. They already knew how to reach China by the long route around the southern tip of Africa. They thought it might be closer to go through North America to China.

Around 1620 the French who lived in Quebec sent a young man named Etienne Brulé to explore the west and look for a route to China. He was about 28 years old. He had been living with the Indians in Canada for about 12 years.

Brulé took along a friend, Grenoble, and a group of Indians. They paddled their canoes through Georgian Bay into Lake Huron. Then they entered the rocky St. Mary's River and went past the place where Sault Ste. Marie now stands. Finally they reached Lake Superior.

Brulé did not find a route to China. But he became the first white man known to pass through the land that later would be called Michigan.

Brulé reported his discoveries to the governor of New France, Samuel de Champlain. Then Brulé went back to live in the Canadian woods. He never again returned to Quebec.

Champlain sent others, like Jean Nicolet, to find the route to China. None were successful. But the Indians gave them a reason to stay in the West—furs!

THE FUR TRADE AND THE INDIANS

Before Cadillac founded Detroit, only a few hundred Frenchmen lived in the Michigan forests. Some were missionaries, some were soldiers and some were fur traders.

Fur trading brought the French huge profits. In Europe, men wore tall, felt hats. The felt was made from beaver fur. Other furs were used for clothes. In North America the Indians had killed animals for food and clothes. Now they began to kill them to trade for other things—guns, knives, hatchets, cloth blankets and iron cooking pots.

The more the Indians acquired European weapons and goods, the more they depended on Europeans. This dependence greatly changed the Indians' way of life. Originally, each Indian family provided its own food, clothing, housing, tools and weapons. Now they began to rely on other people for some of these things.

Sometimes the French fur traders and soldiers gave the Indians brandy and rum for their furs. The French missionaries who lived with the Indians did not like this. They knew that liquor was not good for the Indians.

Cadillac was among those who gave the Indians liquor. He and others said they had to provide liquor in order to compete with the British for good Indian furs. The British would give the Indians liquor even if the French did not.

It is believed that Indians first accepted liquor because it gave them dreams and visions. The Indians based their religion on dreams and visions. They had those dreams and visions after fasting—going without food for a long time. The white man's rum produced dreams and visions much more quickly than fasting.

Just as harmful as liquor were European diseases. The Indians had never been exposed to measles, smallpox and tuberculosis. They had built up no resistance to these, and many died from them.

THE FUR TRADERS

The first French fur traders were called *coureurs de bois,* woods runners. They went alone or in small groups to trade with Indians. Many married Indian women. Some traded liquor to the Indians.

The missionaries complained to the French government about the liquor and

French voyageurs *paddled giant canoes for large fur-trading companies. The canoes carried things to trade with the Indians and brought furs back to the East.*

the marriages. The French government also did not like settlers to trade for furs instead of starting farms. In order to control the fur trade, the government sometimes tried to force the Indians to come to Montreal to trade their furs. At other times it required each fur trader to get a license, or permit, allowing him to trade with the Indians.

Licenses were hard to get, and some fur traders worked without getting them. As a result, *coureur du bois* became a term sometimes used to describe an illegal trader.

As the fur trade grew, large companies began organizing fur-trading trips. They hired *voyageurs* to paddle the giant canoes that carried goods to the West and brought furs back to Montreal.

Voyageurs paddled for hour after hour. Sometimes they sang songs in time with the stroking of their paddles.

The *voyageurs'* canoes were from 25 to 45 feet long. They were much longer than a large car is today. The *voyageurs* had to be strong to carry the canoes and their loads around waterfalls and rapids.

The French canoes that hauled furs were larger than the bark canoes that the Indians used. It took many strong men constantly paddling to move the canoes and their heavy loads of trading goods or furs. The voyageurs also had to be able to haul bales of furs (right) on foot when they came to a portage. A portage, or carrying place, is a spot where travelers cannot continue by water because of a rapids, a waterfall or the need to change to a different lake or river. The voyageurs had to carry their boats and goods across the portages. This voyageur is using snowshoes to walk on snow without sinking in it. Snowshoes, like canoes, were used by Indians before the Europeans came to North America.

Among the many Jesuit missionaries who came to Michigan, Father Jacques Marquette is the best remembered. He and other missionaries set up missions for the Indians at Sault Ste. Marie and St. Ignace. Father Marquette also explored much of the Great Lakes. This sketch was drawn by another missionary. It shows Father Marquette learning from the Indians about places he had never seen.

THE WORK OF MISSIONARIES

The French missionaries tried to convert the Indians to the Catholic religion, but the Indians had their own beliefs. Many of them saw no reason to follow the missionary's religion. The Indians did not have just one god. They had many. They did not like being told by missionaries that their beliefs were false. To Indians, the new Christian religion did not make much sense. It said very little about the things that were important in the wilderness—animals, trees, rivers, the weather.

The missionaries had to be brave. They had to hunt for their own food. They had to build their own homes and missions. Many could not swim, but they traveled in canoes. Some were more than missionaries. They explored, served as doctors and sometimes traded with the Indians for furs. The Indians respected their courage.

The missionaries kept written records of their experiences. They sent these reports to France to raise support for their work. As a result, we know much about Michigan's early history.

Father Marquette and Louis Jolliet were the first white men to explore the upper Mississippi River. This portrait of Marquette was based on an old painting.

The Jesuit order of the Catholic church conducted most of the French missionary work in Michigan. As early as 1641 Fathers Isaac Jogues and Charles Raymbault held Catholic services at Sault Ste. Marie.

In 1668 the Jesuits built their first mission in Michigan at Sault Ste. Marie. Father Jacques Marquette and Father Claude Dablon constructed a wooden chapel and a house there. They put a long wall around their buildings.

Sault Ste. Marie was a good site for meeting Indians. It was a favorite fishing spot of the Chippewa. But three years later Marquette and Dablon moved the mission south to St. Ignace. They thought they would be safer there from attacks by the unfriendly Sioux Indians from the West.

Father Marquette was also an explorer. He and Louis Jolliet traveled from St. Ignace through Lake Michigan and Illinois to the Mississippi River. They were the first white men to explore the upper three-fourths of the Mississippi.

THE FRENCH IN THE LOWER PENINSULA

To reach Michigan, the French took a northern route. From Montreal, they went by the Ottawa River and Lake Nipissing to Georgian Bay and then into Lake Huron. From there, they went to Lake Superior or Lake Michigan.

No records have been found of any white man going to the Lower Peninsula of Michigan before 1669. A few probably crossed the Straits of Mackinac into the northern tip of the Lower Peninsula, but none of them stayed there.

The French stayed out of the Lower Peninsula because of the Iroquois Indians. The Iroquois were allies of the British. They were enemies of the French and of most of the Indian tribes that lived in Michigan. The Iroquois controlled Lake Ontario and Lake Erie. They kept the French from going through those two lakes.

Eventually the French king sent 1,200 soldiers to America to fight the Iroquois. In 1667, the soldiers forced the Iroquois to sign a peace treaty. After the treaty was signed, the French could travel on Lake Ontario and Lake Erie.

In 1671, at Sault Ste. Marie, François St. Lusson claimed for France all the land around the Great Lakes and much of the interior of North America. St. Lusson's clothes were very fancy for the frontier. However, people in France wore even more ornate clothes.

A FRENCH CEREMONY

On June 14, 1671, the French invited hundreds of Indians to a big, colorful ceremony at Sault Ste. Marie.

They wanted to impress the Indians with their power. They wanted the Indians to side with them against the British. They wanted to proclaim that France owned the great interior of the North American continent.

Indians from fourteen tribes came. Also there were Jesuit priests, fur traders and soldiers.

At the ceremony, François St. Lusson picked up a piece of sod. He wore a colorful, blue French officer's uniform. He lifted his sword and the sod high. Then he claimed for France all the Great Lakes and much of the interior of North America.

The Frenchmen fired their guns and shouted. The Indians joined with shouts of approval. There was, however, one problem. The British claimed the same land. The two great powers would decide who owned the land through war.

LA SALLE'S PLAN

A French officer designed a plan for keeping the British out of New France. He was Robert Cavelier, Sieur de la Salle. He suggested that France build a chain of forts from Montreal through the Great Lakes. The chain would continue down the Mississippi River to the Gulf of Mexico. He himself would explore the full length of the Mississippi to find the sites for these forts.

La Salle gained the king's approval for his plan. But the king said that profits from the

The Griffin *was the first sailing ship on the Great Lakes. It was built in 1679 by Robert Cavelier, Sieur de La Salle to carry furs. It disappeared on the way back to Lake Erie with its first load of furs. No one ever found out what happened to it.*

fur trade must pay for the cost of building the forts and operating them. This meant that the fur trade would have to grow.

In 1679 La Salle built a small ship, the *Griffin*, to carry the many furs he hoped to find. The *Griffin* was the first sailing ship on the Great Lakes. With La Salle aboard, it sailed from the east end of Lake Erie in August 1679. At the entrance to Green Bay, on the west side of Lake Michigan, the crew loaded the *Griffin* with furs for the return trip. La Salle got off the ship because he had another mission to accomplish.

The *Griffin* never reached Lake Erie. It became the first Great Lakes mystery ship. To this day, no one knows what happened to it.

La Salle went on to the mouth of the St. Joseph River. There he built Fort Miami and started the first white settlement in the Lower Peninsula.

CADILLAC ASKS TO BUILD A FORT

La Salle's plan for a string of forts was eventually carried out. At various times, the French built seven outposts in Michigan. Some, like Fort St. Joseph at Port Huron, were used for only a few years. Others, like Fort Pontchartrain at Detroit, became major settlements. Cadillac was involved with two of these forts.

In 1694 Cadillac became the commander at Fort de Buade at St. Ignace. Cadillac traded for furs himself and allowed fur traders to give liquor to the Indians. This angered the missionaries at St. Ignace.

The missionaries complained to church leaders and to the king. They asked that the

Indians be protected from the traders. At the same time, too many furs were being shipped to Europe. Few people wanted to buy them, and prices fell.

So, in 1696, King Louis XIV closed the Great Lakes and the Mississippi area to all Frenchmen except missionaries. Fur traders could not go there. The king said the Indians would have to take their furs to Montreal.

Cadillac was angry. He went to Quebec and then to France. He convinced people, including the king, that the French should build a new fort on the banks of the Detroit River. Fur traders, Indians, missionaries and farmers would live at the fort.

Pleased with his victory, Cadillac went back to Montreal. He gathered men, equipment and supplies. Then he, his nine-year-old son, fifty workmen, fifty soldiers, one hundred Indians and two priests set out for the Detroit River.

The group arrived at the Detroit River in July 1701. The small fort they built at Detroit had a wooden wall 12 feet high. They named it Fort Pontchartrain after France's colonial minister. Inside were log houses and a church named St. Anne's.

Cadillac invited Indians to settle near the area. Four Indian groups accepted his invitation. Soon Chippewa, Ottawa, Miami and Wyandot Indians were camped by the fort.

The French farmers who came to Detroit were called *habitants*. They were given land to use, but not to own. In return, they had to pay rent in crops, furs or cash. This system of holding land was called feudalism. The plots of land were long strips. Today we call them ribbon farms.

Cadillac stayed in Detroit only ten years. Some people criticized the way he ran the fort, and in 1711, the king transferred him to Louisiana.

THE FRENCH FIGHT THE BRITISH

The French got along well with many Indian tribes. They did not get along with the British. The two countries were enemies in Europe. In North America, British colonists settled on land the French claimed. French fur traders competed with British fur traders from New York and Hudson Bay.

Around 1715 the French strengthened their posts at Niles and Mackinac. Both would be needed. Between 1689 and 1760, France and Great Britain fought four wars in Europe and North America.

The last war started in 1754. It was called the Seven Years' War in Europe and the French and Indian War in America. No battles were fought in Michigan. The French moved men and supplies from Michigan to battle in other places.

The British won in North America by capturing Quebec and Montreal. In 1763 France and Great Britain signed a peace treaty. France gave up all her land east of the Mississippi River to Great Britain.

British soldiers took over Fort Pontchartrain in November 1760. The French soldiers and government officials left. But the French farmers, fur traders and priests stayed. For the next sixty years, they formed most of Michigan's non-Indian population.

CONCLUSION

In 1622 the French came to Michigan looking for a route to China. Instead they found animals that had valuable fur. So they started the fur trade. The French also brought Christianity and colonists to Michigan.

The fur trade gave the Indians new tools, but it also made them more dependent on other people. No longer did they provide all of their own food, clothes, tools and weapons.

French missionaries tried to help and understand the Indians. They protested using liquor in the fur trade. But they brought new diseases to the Indians, and they weakened the Indians' religious beliefs.

The French first explored the Upper Peninsula. They did not begin their settlement at Detroit until 1701. That year the first white women came to Michigan.

The French and the British fought in North America many times. The French finally lost. They gave up New France, including Michigan, in 1763. Michigan no longer had a French government, but it still had many French people and French traditions.

In the next chapter Michigan Indians will fight the new British government and then make peace with it.

Fort Michilimackinac

Fort Pontchartrain

Fort St. Joseph

THE NEXT STORY

As this chapter starts, British soldiers have just replaced the French in the forts in Michigan. This chapter tells how and why the Indians fought the British and then made peace with them.

PEOPLE

Chief Pontiac was the most famous of the Indian chiefs who fought against the new British rulers. He convinced Indians from three different tribes to join together to attack Detroit.

Major Henry Gladwin commanded the fort at Detroit. He made the Indians angry by not giving them gifts or respect.

PLACES

Fort Pontchartrain (pŏn-chĕr-trān) was the fort at Detroit that Pontiac attacked.

Fort St. Joseph stood beside the St. Joseph River in southwest Michigan south of the present city of Niles. It had few British soldiers and was taken by Indians.

Fort Michilimackinac (mĭsh-ĭ-lă-măk-ĭ-năw) was at the northern tip of the Lower Peninsula. Indians attacked it while pretending to play a game. A reconstruction of it stands just west of the Mackinac Bridge.

WORDS

A **siege** is a type of warfare in which a group surrounds an enemy fort or town to keep it from getting outside food or help until it surrenders.

Palisades are tall walls built around a fort. They are made of a row of large pointed logs stuck deep into the ground.

Wampum belts are made of beads made from shells. Sometimes the Indians used wampum strings and belts as ornaments. They used different colored beads to weave designs. The designs might represent an agreement or tell a story. Wampum belts were exchanged to show sincerity or record treaty agreements.

A **convoy** is a group of ships or other vehicles traveling together to protect each other.

WHEN DID IT HAPPEN?

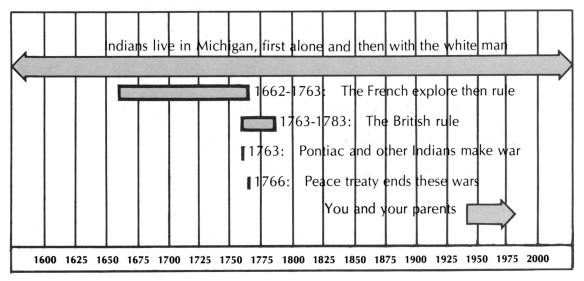

Indians live in Michigan, first alone and then with the white man

1662-1763:   The French explore then rule

1763-1783:   The British rule

1763:   Pontiac and other Indians make war

1766:   Peace treaty ends these wars

You and your parents

| 1600 | 1625 | 1650 | 1675 | 1700 | 1725 | 1750 | 1775 | 1800 | 1825 | 1850 | 1875 | 1900 | 1925 | 1950 | 1975 | 2000 |

CHAPTER THREE
THE INDIANS AND THE BRITISH

Chief Pontiac stood before the large group of Indian warriors. His glowing eyes showed his anger at the British. It was April 27, 1763.

Sitting before Chief Pontiac, the Ottawa warriors were wrapped in their brightly colored blankets. The Huron wore their painted shirts. The Potawatomi rested their light war clubs in their folded arms.

Ten miles away on the shore of the Detroit River stood the white man's settlement—Fort Pontchartrain. British (also called English) soldiers lived there.

To get his warriors as angry as he was, Pontiac began telling them a story about an Indian. This Indian went off to seek the living place of the Indians' Great Spirit. The Great Spirit suddenly appeared before the Indian and said: "Why do you suffer the white man to dwell among you? My child, have you forgotten the customs and traditions of your forefathers? Why do you not clothe yourself in skins, as your forefathers did? And why do you not use the bows and arrows and stone-pointed lances which they used?"

Pontiac was upset because so many Indians had bought guns, knives, kettles and blankets from the white man. These Indians could no longer do without the white man's things.

In Pontiac's tale the Great Spirit kept talking to the Indian: "And as for these English—these dogs dressed in red who have come to rob you of your hunting grounds and drive away the game—you must lift your hatchet against them. Wipe them from the face of the earth! And then you will win my favor back again and once more be happy and prosperous."

By now the warriors understood the point of Pontiac's story. Pontiac then proposed that they attack Fort Pontchartrain. His angry speech produced the longest Indian siege ever made against the white man. It lasted 153 days or almost half a year.

Kelly Nelson

Fort Pontchartrain was built of logs beside the Detroit River. The Indians did not try to climb over the tall walls, but sometimes they fired flaming arrows over them.

For the Indians, such a long siege was almost unbelievable. Each Indian warrior was independent in his thinking. You could not easily talk him into going to war. He had to believe there was a good reason. He had to believe in the person who was acting as leader. He had to believe he could win. It was also hard to get warriors from different tribes to fight together.

But Pontiac was able to get the Indians from three tribes to join together for a very long time. He was a great leader and a great speaker.

WHY PONTIAC WAS ANGRY

The first British commander at Fort Pontchartrain—which later became known as Detroit—was Captain Donald Campbell.

He treated the Indians with respect. He also gave them gifts as the French had done. But in 1762 a new commander, Major Henry Gladwin, took over. He greeted the Indians with frowns and harsh words.

Meanwhile British officials way off in England made new rules for the Indians. But the officials knew little about the Indians' customs and beliefs. The officials said soldiers could not give gifts to Indians. They also said the Indians could not have gunpowder.

In addition, the British had trouble controlling fur traders. Some fur traders began ignoring the British rules about dealing fairly with the Indians. They gave the Indians poor quality goods. That angered the Indians.

Major Henry Gladwin commanded the fort during the 153-day siege by Chief Pontiac.

A British drummer would sound the signal telling soldiers to prepare for action.

What angered the Indians the most was the loss of their land. White settlers were moving into lands south of Michigan. When the Indians fought back, they were called "savages." Today some people still call them savages.

The Indians were not savages ruthlessly killing settlers for the joy of killing. They were defending their way of life. Many Indians died trying to defend their way of life.

One great Indian chief once summed up the feelings of many Indians this way:

"What white man can say I ever stole his land or a penny of his money? Yet they say I am a thief. What white woman, however lonely, was ever captive or insulted by me? Yet they say I am a bad Indian. What white man has ever seen me drunk?

"Who has ever come to me hungry and unfed? Who has ever seen me beat my wives or abuse my children? What law have I broken? Is it wrong for me to love my own? Is it wicked for me because my skin is red, because I am an Indian, because I would die for my people and my country?"

It is important to remember the Indian way of thinking about two things.

One was the land. The Indian loved the land. The Indian thought it was there for all to use. To the Indian, the land was not there for only one person or one group to own.

The second thing was the Indians' sense of freedom. They wanted freedom to rule themselves. When the white man took the Indians' land and freedom away, the Indians fought back.

In the fight that Pontiac led, the Indians thought they would have the support of the French. Some French leaders in America hinted that France might send soldiers to help the Indians. But the French government never did.

PONTIAC ORGANIZES HIS ATTACK

Many different Indian groups organized to resist the new British rulers.

Of all the Indians' efforts against the British, the biggest was Pontiac's siege at Detroit. Pontiac knew his Indians would have a hard time attacking the fort directly. Tall, heavy, wooden palisades protected it. Inside these walls were houses, shops and barracks.

So Pontiac planned a trick. He politely asked if he could meet the fort's commander, Major Henry Gladwin, inside the fort at a peace council. Major Gladwin agreed to the meeting.

On May 7, 1763, Pontiac with ten chiefs and about sixty warriors showed up at the fort. Hidden beneath their blankets, the Indians carried knives, tomahawks and guns.

Chief Pontiac himself was carrying a wampum belt. Wampum belts were important in making peace treaties. They reminded people of their promises. Pontiac's belt was white on one side and green on the other. The two different colors were part of Pontiac's trick.

Beforehand, he had told his Indians that if he turned up the green side when he handed it to the major, his Indians were to attack the British soldiers. The white side meant they should not attack.

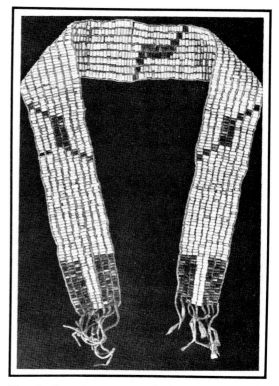

The Indians' wampum belt made of shell beads took the place of a written document in a peace treaty.

When Pontiac's men entered the fort, they were surprised to find the British prepared. Alert soldiers stood all around the fort. Guns rested on their shoulders. Somehow Major Gladwin had learned of Pontiac's secret plan.

So Pontiac played it safe. When it came time to give the wampum belt to Gladwin, Pontiac showed the white side—and not the green. The Indians quietly left.

Later Pontiac returned to the fort's gate with other chiefs and tribesmen. The fort commander said only Pontiac and a few chiefs could enter. Pontiac refused to enter unless he could take all his men in. He angrily left the gate.

At dawn the next day the Indians began their 153-day siege. They hid behind small buildings and barns, behind fences and small hills. From there they fired their guns and arrows. Sometimes they shot flaming arrows over the walls. They aimed at the roofs of buildings to set them on fire. The British had to keep buckets of water everywhere.

The British knew they had one advantage: the fort was right beside the river. The British could have supplies brought in by boat.

THE DAY THE FIRST BOATS CAME

For nearly three weeks no boats came. The soldiers and settlers inside became very tired. Finally on the morning of May 30 a joyful sight greeted them. A convoy of small boats was moving up the river, oars flashing in the sun. The first boat flew the red flag of England. Inside the fort the soldiers cheered.

Suddenly the soldiers stopped celebrating. They gasped—horror-struck. Rising from the bottoms of the boats were dark, wildly-painted Indians. It turned out that the convoy had been attacked and captured by the Indians as it left Lake Erie and started up the river. The fort got no supplies.

On July 20 a second convoy of small British boats made it safely. In addition to food and supplies, it carried about 260 soldiers.

On the night of July 31 the British decided to come out of the fort and attack the Indian camps. While the British were boldly marching down a road, the Indians hid behind trees, bushes and buildings. Suddenly the Indians attacked. They killed or wounded about 60 of the 250 British soldiers. The stream where the Indians attacked the British came to be known as Bloody Run.

This victory excited the Indians. It renewed their interest in the long siege. But for Pontiac, it was the last great effort. As the siege moved into the autumn of 1763, the Indians became less interested. More and more of them moved away. Finally on October 31 Pontiac ended the siege. He moved south to Ohio.

OTHER INDIAN ATTACKS

Other Indian groups attacked other British forts from Michigan to Pennsylvania and New York. Eventually they captured all the British forts except three—Fort Pontchartrain, Fort Pitt in Pennsylvania and Fort Niagara in New York State.

People used to think Pontiac planned all these attacks. They called the battles "Pontiac's Conspiracy." But historians now agree it was not a conspiracy. The other Indian groups acted independently. All were upset at the way the British were treating them and the way the settlers were moving onto their land. They often knew about each other, but they did not have a single leader telling them what to do.

One of the Indian attacks took place at the little stockade on the St. Joseph River in southwestern Michigan, called Fort St. Joseph. There, Ensign Francis Schlosser commanded 15 men.

The painting at top shows the scene at Fort Michilimackinac on June 2, 1763. The Indians were playing a game called baggata-way. British soldiers came out of the fort to watch. The soldiers left the fort's gate open. Indian women standing along the wall hid weapons beneath their blankets. Suddenly the Indians grabbed the weapons from the women and rushed at the soldiers. The Indians captured the fort. They killed 25 soldiers and a fur trader. The state has built a replica of the fort. Every Memorial Day weekend, people reenact the Indians' capturing of the fort. The bottom photo shows a recent reenactment.

On May 25, about three weeks after the siege began at Detroit, the Potawatomi Indians asked to meet with Ensign Schlosser inside Fort St. Joseph. The commander was not suspicious. He agreed to meet Chief Washashe and three or four other Indians in his quarters.

They had hardly begun talking when the commander heard noises outside. Rushing out, he found the fort was being taken over by other Indians who had been allowed inside the walls. Nine British soldiers were killed. Schlosser and others were captured. They later were exchanged for Indian captives at Detroit.

Another Indian attack took place at Fort Michilimackinac on June 2, 1763. It was a warm, sunny day. The British soldiers were celebrating the king's birthday. The Chippewa Indians had convinced the British to invite them to the celebration.

Everyone—whites and Indians, men and women—had gathered outside the fort. They were watching two Indian tribes play a game in which both sides kicked and threw the ball using sticks with woven baskets on one end.

Meanwhile the soldiers left the gates to the fort wide open. Indian women, blankets slung across their shoulders, were watching the game. As time went on, the women moved closer to the gate. What the soldiers did not know was that the women had hidden weapons beneath their blankets.

Suddenly an Indian player threw the ball over the fort wall. All the players dashed toward the gates. Immediately the women handed them their weapons. Quickly the Indians ran through the gates and captured the fort. They killed 25 soldiers and one British fur trader. They also captured supplies and prisoners.

In Michigan and elsewhere, the Indians fought bravely against the British and sometimes won. But the British were too powerful and kept the most important forts. Finally the British and the Indians signed a peace treaty in 1766 at Oswego, New York. One of the chiefs who signed was Pontiac. Afterwards he asked other Indians to live in peace with the British.

Meanwhile the British did some things so they could get along better with the Indians. The British tried to improve fur-trading practices. They also tried to limit white settlement.

In a strange twist of fate, Pontiac was murdered in 1769 in Illinois. The chief who led the Indians' longest siege against the white man was murdered not by a white man but by an Indian.

CONCLUSION

The Indian attacks that took place in Michigan and other areas in the 1760s indicated three important things:

1. The Indians did not like the change from French to British rule and actively opposed it.
2. The Indians had the will and the ability to fight and defend their rights, especially their land.
3. The British had better weapons and supplies and won the important battles against the Indians.

In the next chapter the British face a new war, this time with the white colonists who declare their independence.

THE NEXT STORY

In this chapter Michigan becomes a territory of the United States. It plays a small part in the American Revolution and a larger part in the War of 1812. Between the wars, the Indians give up some of their Michigan land, and the Americans make plans for the Northwest Territory, which includes Michigan.

PEOPLE

David and Elizabeth Mitchell lived on Mackinac Island. He was a British officer, and she was his part-Indian wife.

Lieutenant Governor Henry Hamilton was a British officer at Detroit. During the American Revolution he paid Indians for the scalps of Americans.

General Anthony Wayne, an American general, defeated the Indians at the Battle of Fallen Timbers.

William Hull was the first governor of the Michigan Territory. He surrendered Detroit to the British in 1812.

Oliver Hazard Perry commanded the American naval ships that defeated the British on Lake Erie during the War of 1812.

• Mackinac Island
• Fort Michilimackinac

Fort Lernoult •

Fort St. Joseph •
Frenchtown •

PLACES

Mackinac Island is in Lake Huron, east of Fort Michilimackinac. The British moved there during the American Revolution.

Fort Lernoult was built at Detroit by the British during the American Revolution. Its name was later changed to Fort Shelby.

Frenchtown is now called Monroe. The Battle of the River Raisin was fought there in 1813.

WORDS

The American Revolution is also called the **Revolutionary War** and the **War of Independence.** In it the American colonists fought for and won their freedom from Great Britain.

To cede is to give up or transfer something.

A **territory** was a part of the United States that did not have enough people to be a state. The president of the United States appointed a territory's governor. He was not elected.

The **West** at this time meant the land that was west of the Appalachian Mountains. It included such places as Kentucky, Ohio, Michigan and Illinois.

The **Northwest Territory** included Michigan and the area around it. In 1787 Congress drew up a plan called the **Northwest Ordinance** to govern this territory.

The **War of 1812** was the second major conflict between Great Britain and the United States.

WHEN DID IT HAPPEN?

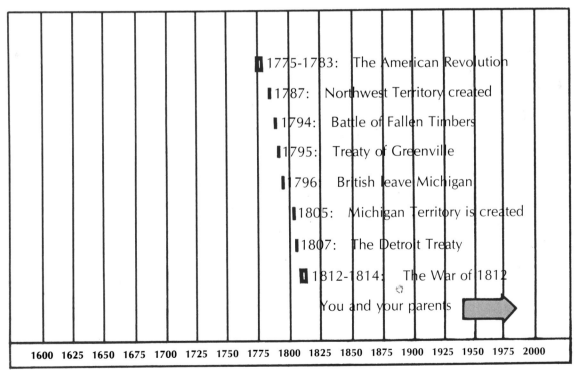

1775-1783: The American Revolution

1787: Northwest Territory created

1794: Battle of Fallen Timbers

1795: Treaty of Greenville

1796: British leave Michigan

1805: Michigan Territory is created

1807: The Detroit Treaty

1812-1814: The War of 1812

You and your parents

| 1600 | 1625 | 1650 | 1675 | 1700 | 1725 | 1750 | 1775 | 1800 | 1825 | 1850 | 1875 | 1900 | 1925 | 1950 | 1975 | 2000 |

42

CHAPTER FOUR
BETWEEN TWO WARS, MICHIGAN BECOMES A TERRITORY

It was Christmas Day 1780. Americans had been fighting for their independence from Great Britain for five years. In what is now Michigan, the British were moving from Fort Michilimackinac to Mackinac Island. They thought the island would be easier to defend.

David Mitchell was a doctor in the British Army. He had already moved into his large house on Market Street on Mackinac Island.

Elizabeth had many friends at Mackinac. But David was afraid that people who lived on the East Coast of America and in Britain would dislike her because she was part Indian and different from them. Many soldiers and fur traders who married Indian women left their wives behind when they went east.

Finally David knew what he must do. He took out a piece of paper, a quill pen and some ink and wrote to his commander: "My circumstances . . . make it very detrimental to my interest to leave this post with the Regiment . . . I hope I may be allow'd to resign." David would stay with Elizabeth.

David and Elizabeth became prosperous fur traders, farmers and merchants. They had a dozen children and lived on or near Mackinac Island for the next fifty years. When David had to leave the island, Elizabeth ran their business.

This is how Detroit looked in 1794. It had not changed much since the American Revolution. The British still ruled and many of the people who lived there still spoke French. The fort beside the Detroit River stood about where Cobo Hall now stands.

THE AMERICAN REVOLUTION

When the British first sent David to Mackinac, the Revolutionary War was just starting. Michigan was not a state or even a territory. It was part of a large frontier area called the West.

Americans in the thirteen British colonies on the East Coast wanted to settle the West. The British wanted to avoid problems with the Indians. They tried to keep settlers from moving west.

The British also wanted the American colonists to help pay for governing the West. So they taxed the Americans. The Americans did not want to pay taxes unless they had a say in how the money would be spent.

Because of these and other disagreements between the British and their American colonies, the Americans declared their independence from Great Britain. Britain tried to force them to remain colonies. The result was the American Revolution.

THE REVOLUTION IN MICHIGAN

The American Revolution began in 1775. Michigan did not play a big part. The British held Michigan throughout the Revolution and used it as a base for raids elsewhere.

Though the Indians had fought the British twenty years earlier, they helped the British during the American Revolution. Like the British, they did not want American colonists to settle the West.

To get the Indians' help, the British paid money for each white person's scalp that the Indians brought to the fort in Detroit. The British also paid money for white captives. The British commander at Detroit was Lieutenant Governor Henry Hamilton. Among Americans he was known as the "Hair Buyer." Hamilton did not actively encourage the killing of Americans. But he had to keep the Indians as allies and bought the scalps in order not to anger them. The Indians attacked American settlements all over the West.

During the American Revolution, Great Britain ruled Michigan. There were no battles in Michigan, but British soldiers held the forts at Detroit and the Straits of Mackinac. Some of the British soldiers wore red-coated uniforms like the one at right. The British commander at Detroit was Henry Hamilton (above). He and the other British soldiers encouraged Michigan Indians to fight the Americans. The Indians and the British both wanted to keep the Americans from settling in the West.

45

One of the wooden-hulled British boats that sailed in the Straits of Mackinac 200 years ago was the Welcome. *In the 1970s, this replica of it was built.*

On one of their raids into Kentucky, the Shawnee Indians captured Daniel Boone. They brought him to Detroit where the British offered to buy him. The Indians refused and took Boone to Ohio, where he later escaped.

Meanwhile, one American, Lieutenant Colonel George Rogers Clark, thought he knew how to halt the Indian attacks. He planned to capture British forts, like Detroit, so that they could no longer be used as bases for Indian attacks.

Clark won several key battles south and east of Michigan in 1778 and 1779. The French, who fought on the side of the Americans, helped Clark.

The British feared that Clark would attack Michigan. So they built Fort Lernoult in Detroit where the Federal Building now stands on Lafayette Boulevard. They also moved from Fort Michilimackinac to a new fort on Mackinac Island. However, Clark was unable to gather enough men and equipment to invade Michigan.

The British built the fort on Mackinac Island. Later the Americans occupied it. Now restored, Fort Mackinac is one of Michigan's most popular tourist attractions.

Spain also joined the Americans in fighting the British. Spain owned the area west of the Mississippi River. In December 1780 Spanish troops left Missouri for Fort St. Joseph near Niles. They thought that British soldiers were there, but the fort was empty when they arrived in February 1781.

The Spanish flag flew over the fort for one day before the troops left. Niles became known as the "City of Four Flags"—French, British, Spanish and American.

The British and the Americans fought many battles between 1775 and 1781. In October 1781, in the war's last major battle, British General Lord Cornwallis surren-

dered to American General George Washington at Yorktown, Virginia.

The British people were tired of the high cost of the war in far off America. Finally, in 1783, British and American officials signed the peace treaty that ended the American Revolution.

The peace treaty gave the territory west of the Appalachians, including Michigan, to the United States. But the British refused to leave the forts at Detroit and Mackinac Island. They said they were staying because the Americans did not do all they promised to do in the peace treaty. But the British also stayed to protect their fur trade.

Under the Ordinance of 1785, frontier land was divided into squares called sections before it was sold. Those squares, often marked by roads today, explain why much of Michigan looks like a checkerboard when seen from the air.

THE NORTHWEST TERRITORY

After the peace treaty, Congress passed several laws affecting United States territory in the Great Lakes area. The most important was the Northwest Ordinance of 1787. It created the Northwest Territory.

The territory stretched from Pennsylvania's western border to the Mississippi River. It went from the border with Canada to the Ohio River. Michigan, Ohio, Indiana, Illinois, Wisconsin and part of Minnesota were in the Northwest Territory.

In 1785, another ordinance had said that the land was to be divided up into squares before it was sold. If you fly over Michigan today, you can see roads along the squares

created under this plan. That ordinance also set aside land for schools.

The Northwest Ordinance said that no less than three and no more than five states should be created from the territory. A region first became a separate territory with an appointed governor. When a territory had a population of at least 60,000 "free" persons it could ask Congress to make it a state. Indians and slaves were not counted as "free" people. The Northwest Ordinance banned slavery in the territory. The few people who already had slaves there were allowed to keep them, but slavery soon disappeared from the Northwest Territory.

After the 1783 British-American peace treaty ending the American Revolution, the Americans and the Indians kept on fighting. Finally President George Washington sent General Anthony Wayne to the West. Wayne won a decisive victory in 1794 at the Battle of Fallen Timbers south of Toledo, Ohio. In 1796, Wayne commanded the American troops that took over Detroit. Wayne County is named after him.

THE INDIANS STILL FIGHT

After the peace treaty between Britain and the United States, the Indians kept fighting to keep the white settlers off their land. To stop these attacks, President George Washington sent General Anthony Wayne to Ohio. He was called "Mad" Anthony Wayne because he was sometimes reckless and daring.

On August 20, 1794, the forces of General Wayne and Chief Blue Jacket met south of present-day Toledo, Ohio, in the Battle of Fallen Timbers. It was called that because a tornado had ripped down the trees.

The Indians expected help from British soldiers in a nearby fort. But no help came, and Wayne won. For the time being, British and Indian efforts to keep Americans out of Ohio and Michigan had ended.

In the summer of 1795 the Indians and General Wayne signed a peace treaty at Greenville, Ohio. The Indians agreed to cede, or transfer by treaty, to the Americans almost all of Ohio and some of Indiana and Michigan. The Michigan land included Mackinac Island and small areas along the Detroit River and the Straits of Mackinac. For the land, the Indians received goods valued at $20,000 and a promise of $9,500 worth of goods each year.

In 1796 the British left the lands the Indians had ceded to the United States. On July 11, 1796, the American army arrived in Detroit. On September 1, 1796, the Americans occupied Mackinac Island.

David and Elizabeth Mitchell again had a problem. They did not know whether to leave with the British or stay. They stayed, but they remained citizens of Great Britain.

This is how an artist pictured the Indians and Americans at the signing of the Treaty of Greenville, Ohio, in 1795. The Indians ceded land at Detroit and Mackinac.

About a year later, the British agreed to leave Detroit and Mackinac Island. Here, the Americans are raising their flag at Mackinac.

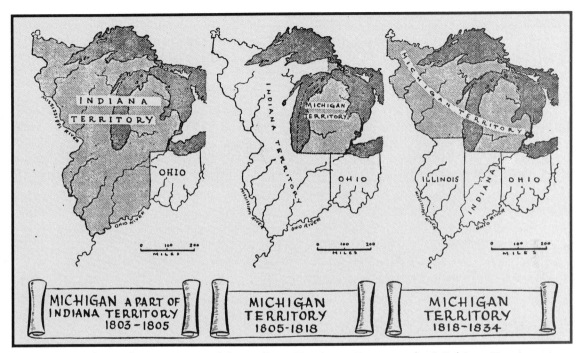

In 1803, Michigan became part of the Indiana Territory. But soon the Michigan Territory was created. Eventually two states and a part of a third were formed from these lands.

MICHIGAN TERRITORY CREATED

Michigan finally became a place that could be located on maps in 1805. However, it was a territory, not a state. At first it included only a small part of the Upper Peninsula. In 1818 it grew to include Wisconsin and part of Minnesota.

In 1805 the new Michigan Territory had only 3,000 white people. Most of the land belonged to the Indians. Because very little land was for sale, few pioneers came to Michigan. To get more land, the U.S. government told Michigan Territorial Governor William Hull to negotiate with the Indians.

On November 17, 1807, the chiefs from the Ottawa, Chippewa, Potawatomi and Huron met with Hull at Detroit and signed the Detroit Treaty. It was the first treaty involving a lot of Michigan land. The Indians ceded a large part of southeastern Michigan. The United States government gave the Indians $10,000 in goods and money and promised to give them $2,400 a year. The Indians also kept the right to hunt and fish on the land.

At this time there were only four towns within the Michigan Territory. They were Detroit, Sault Ste. Marie, Mackinac Island and Frenchtown (now called Monroe). With a population of about one thousand, Detroit was the largest. Many of its people still spoke French.

Mackinac Island had several hundred permanent residents. But in the summer several thousand Indians and fur traders gathered there to do business. The Straits of Mackinac had been a center of the Great Lakes fur trade since the time when the French ruled Michigan.

Independent fur traders, like David and Elizabeth Mitchell, did much of the trading under British and American rule. However in 1808 John Jacob Astor and his American Fur Company came to Mackinac Island. Astor forced many of the independent traders out of business by paying high prices for furs. By 1811 he controlled most of the Great Lakes fur trade. No one worried about killing too many animals in those days. As beavers became hard to find in Michigan, the fur traders went farther west where there were still plenty of wild animals.

THE WAR OF 1812

In 1812, Great Britain and the United States declared war on each other. There were many causes.

Great Britain and France were at war with each other. France had been keeping American ships from trading with Great Britain. Great Britain had been keeping American ships from trading with France. France agreed to stop doing this, but Britain did not.

The British also claimed that British sailors were serving on American ships. When they stopped an American ship, they often "impressed" British and American sailors. That means they forced them to serve on British ships.

At the same time Americans blamed the British in Canada for Indian uprisings in the Ohio River Valley. Canada was still a British colony. A Shawnee Indian chief named Tecumseh led the uprisings.

On June 18, 1812, the U.S. Congress declared war on Great Britain. The United States Army had only 7,000 soldiers, and the Navy had only sixteen large ships. Most of the British Army and Navy were being used to fight France in Europe. Canadian and American volunteers fought much of the war in America.

The British also had help from Indians. These Indians thought of themselves as allies of the British. They did not always do what the British told them to do. The British sometimes used this fact to frighten the Americans.

On July 12, 1812, Governor Hull, newly appointed general of the Northwestern Army, invaded Canada from Detroit. He set up a camp where Windsor is now and prepared to go farther. Later, after he learned that the British had captured Mackinac and were sending troops to the Detroit area, he decided to retreat. He returned to Detroit on August 8.

General Isaac Brock led a British army of 1,350 men. About half of the people in Brock's army were Indians.

Brock decided to try to capture Detroit. On August 15 he sent Hull a message warning that "The numerous Indians who have attached themselves to my troops will be beyond my control the moment the contest begins."

With an army of about 1,600 men, Hull responded that he was ready to meet any

British General Isaac Brock (top left) and Indian leader Tecumseh (top right) forced American General William Hull to surrender Detroit in August 1812. After the United States reoccupied the city in 1814, men like William Woodbridge (left) worked to make Detroit and the Michigan Territory better places to live. Woodbridge arrived in the Michigan Territory in 1814. He was the territorial secretary. He eventually served Michigan as governor, U.S. senator, territorial delegate to Congress, Michigan Supreme Court justice and delegate to the 1835 Michigan constitutional convention. Woodbridge died in Detroit in 1861.

British force. From across the river the British fired their cannon on Detroit. The Americans fired back.

During the night the British crossed the river south of Detroit. In the morning the British cannon fired while the British army advanced on the fort. Fearing that the Indians with the British might massacre civilians at Detroit. Hull surrendered without fighting.

Later the army found Hull guilty of cowardice, neglect of duty and unofficer-like conduct. He was sentenced to be shot. President James Madison prevented his execution.

Some historians say Hull's surrender prevented an Indian massacre and that he had no other choice. Others believe he should have fought the British.

CAPTURE OF MACKINAC ISLAND

During the first week Hull was in Canada, the British sent six hundred men to seize Mackinac Island. David Mitchell was among them. He had left Mackinac Island to join the British army as a hospital mate.

Fort Mackinac is on the south side of the island. About 3:00 A.M. on July 17, the British and Indians landed secretly on the island's north shore. They pulled two cannons to the top of a hill that overlooked the fort. The next morning Lieutenant Porter Hanks and sixty-one American soldiers surrendered without firing a shot.

REMEMBER THE RIVER RAISIN

One of the war's most tragic battles took place where the River Raisin enters Lake Erie at Frenchtown, now called Monroe.

Fearing an Indian massacre, General William Hull (above) surrendered Detroit to the British in 1812 without a fight.

The Americans had about 1,000 soldiers camped there on the night of January 21, 1813. Just before dawn they were surprised by a larger British force.

Some of the Americans surrrendered, while others fought. The British commander warned the Americans that they should give up. He said that if they did not give up, the Indians could not be kept from killing the American prisoners. The Americans surrendered, and the British promised that they would protect the Americans from the Indians.

However, the British commander, Henry Proctor, feared that more American soldiers would arrive, so he retreated to Fort Malden across the Detroit River. He took all of his

54

In the Battle of Lake Erie in 1813, Lieutenant Oliver Perry's flagship, the Lawrence, *was destroyed. Most of its crewmen were killed or wounded, but Perry was unhurt. He rowed to the* Niagara *and continued to fight. This painting shows him boarding the* Niagara.

soldiers and the American prisoners who could walk. They left behind the other wounded, the townsfolk and two British Army doctors.

Early the next morning, about two hundred Indians rushed into the village and killed many of the wounded. Many of those killed were from Kentucky. In Kentucky and elsewhere the angry war cry became "Remember the River Raisin."

A GREAT NAVAL BATTLE

In March 1813, Lieutenant Oliver Hazard Perry arrived at what is now Erie, Pennsylvania, to assemble a fleet of American ships for the Great Lakes. He was to try to take control of the lakes away from the British. He had four ships. In five months, five more were built. On August 1, 1813, Perry's fleet moved westward through Lake Erie toward the Detroit River.

Perry's fleet sailed the length of the lake without finding the British fleet. Finally, near the mouth of the Detroit River, Perry sighted six British ships. They were guarded by the guns of Britain's Fort Malden and refused to come out and fight. Perry sailed back to Put-in-Bay near where Cedar Point Amusement Park is today. He anchored his ships there and waited.

Early on the morning of September 10, the Americans spotted six British ships moving toward them. Perry's fleet moved out to meet the British.

The house above was one of the finest homes on Mackinac Island when David and Elizabeth Mitchell lived in it. It was run down but still standing in the 1890s, when this photo was taken. The painting at left shows an Ottawa Indian woman in clothing like Elizabeth Mitchell might have worn on Mackinac Island. According to one written description, Elizabeth was tall and stout. She always wore black, usually silk. On her head, she wore a plumed black beaver-felt hat.

As the warships approached each other Perry hoisted a blue flag on his ship, the *Lawrence,* which read, "Don't Give Up The Ship." It was Perry's signal to attack.

For over two hours the ships fought. The *Lawrence* was destroyed. Most of its crew were killed or wounded. With his ship sinking, Perry, who was unhurt, took his flag down and rowed to the *Niagara.* He ordered the *Niagara* and his smaller ships to attack the center of the British fleet.

Three hours and fifteen minutes after the battle started the British surrendered. Perry wrote to American General William Henry Harrison, "We have met the enemy and they are ours."

The Americans now controlled all the Great Lakes except Lake Ontario. The British knew that they could no longer hold the fort at Detroit and retreated toward Toronto. Nineteen days after Perry's victory, the American army entered Detroit.

PEACE COMES

The war dragged on through 1814. Both sides became tired of fighting. Neither thought it could win easily. Peace negotiations began. On December 24, 1814, British and American leaders at Ghent, Belgium, signed a peace treaty.

The Americans peacefully moved back onto Mackinac Island in 1815. But it was not easy for people to forget the war. David Mitchell, now sixty-five, had fought with the British. When the British went to nearby Drummond Island, he went with them. Elizabeth Mitchell planned to stay at Mackinac and manage their businesses. However, she too went to Drummond for a while because the Americans distrusted her. After feelings cooled down, Elizabeth returned to Mackinac. She visited David from time to time until her death in 1827. David died in 1832.

CONCLUSION

From 1775 to 1815 Michigan remained a frontier area. It did not become a territory until 1805. The fur trade dominated its economy. Most of its people were Indians.

Michigan was important in the American Revolution (1775-1783) as part of the western area that American colonists and the British government disagreed about.

Because Michigan was a frontier area and close to the British territory called Canada, it was hard for the Americans to take control of it. There were three examples of this:

1. The American government passed the Northwest Ordinance in 1787 to govern Michigan and its neighbors, but the British did not leave Detroit and Mackinac until 1796.
2. The Indians fought against settlement and sometimes helped the British. They did not sign their first treaty with the Americans ceding land in Michigan until 1795.
3. In the War of 1812 the British took Detroit and Mackinac again. They had to give up Detroit after Oliver Perry won control of Lake Erie.

After the War of 1812, Michigan was firmly under American control and ready for pioneers to come. The next chapter tells how thousands came to Michigan to start farms and businesses.

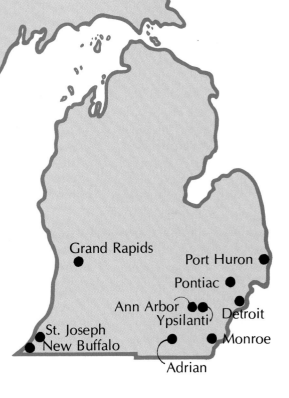

Sault Ste. Marie

Grand Rapids

Port Huron

Pontiac

Ann Arbor

Ypsilanti

Detroit

St. Joseph

New Buffalo

Monroe

Adrian

THE NEXT STORY

As this chapter starts, the United States finally is governing Michigan. This chapter tells how Lewis Cass set out to prove that Michigan could be a good place in which to live. It also tells how making treaties with the Indians and getting better transportation brought pioneers to Michigan.

PEOPLE

Lewis Cass was governor of the Michigan Territory from 1813 to 1831. He encouraged people to settle there.

Neenay Johnston helped persuade the Indians to accept Cass's plans.

Chief Sassaba was a Chippewa Indian who opposed one of Cass's plans in 1820.

Speckled Snake wanted to stay in Michigan when the U.S. government wanted the Indians to move west in 1829.

PLACES

Sault Ste. Marie, also called the Soo, was where Cass built a fort.

Adrian was at the end of the first railroad in Michigan.

Monroe, Pontiac and **Port Huron** were the first towns linked to **Detroit** by roads.

Ypsilanti and **Ann Arbor** were along the road that was built to Chicago, Illinois.

New Buffalo, St. Joseph and **Grand Rapids** were to be linked to the eastern part of the state by railroads.

Michigan Territory at first (1805) included the Lower Peninsula and part of the Upper Peninsula. Land was added until in 1834 it reached the Missouri River in North Dakota.

WORDS

A **geologist** studies rocks and other things that tell him how the earth was made.

An **interpreter** is used when people who speak different languages meet. The interpreter can speak both languages and explains to each person what the other is saying.

The **Saginaw Treaty** was between the Chippewa and Ottawa Indians and the United States. The Indians ceded most of the east-central part of the Lower Peninsula to the United States.

Indian **reservations** are lands set aside just for use by the Indians.

WHEN DID IT HAPPEN?

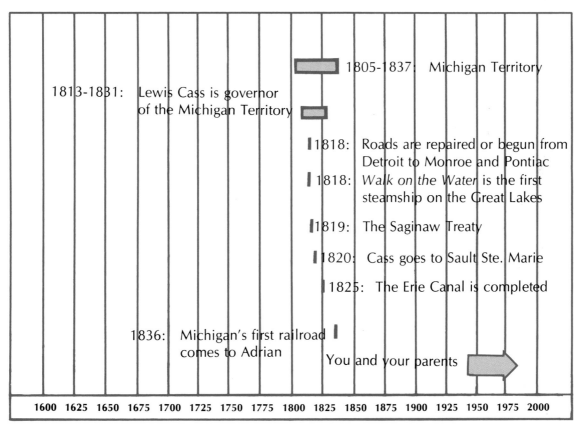

1813-1831: Lewis Cass is governor of the Michigan Territory

1805-1837: Michigan Territory

1818: Roads are repaired or begun from Detroit to Monroe and Pontiac

1818: *Walk on the Water* is the first steamship on the Great Lakes

1819: The Saginaw Treaty

1820: Cass goes to Sault Ste. Marie

1825: The Erie Canal is completed

1836: Michigan's first railroad comes to Adrian

You and your parents

| 1600 | 1625 | 1650 | 1675 | 1700 | 1725 | 1750 | 1775 | 1800 | 1825 | 1850 | 1875 | 1900 | 1925 | 1950 | 1975 | 2000 |

CHAPTER FIVE
CASS EXPLORES
THE MICHIGAN TERRITORY

In 1820 Lewis Cass was governor of the Michigan Territory. He and 42 men in three big canoes were paddling up the St. Mary's River. Cass had begun a trip around the territory. He was trying to find out whether the land was good for people to live on.

At the head of the river—where Sault Ste. Marie now stands—Cass and his men tied up their canoes. They set up tents. That area interested Cass because it was still a major fur-trading place. He wanted to build a fort there.

Cass called some Chippewa Indian chiefs to his tent. He told them his plans for the fort. Cass said that a treaty the Indians had signed 25 years before gave the United States the right to build a fort there. That morning Cass asked the chiefs to approve this new fort.

The Indians told Cass they did not want the fort. Cass looked at them sternly. He pointed to the sun and said, "As sure as the sun will set, there will be an American fort built here."

Sitting among the Indians was Chief Sassaba. He still wore the red coat of a British officer's uniform. Sassaba shouted that Cass was no good. He jumped up and kicked away all the presents Cass had brought. Then he hurried out of the tent. The other chiefs followed him.

A little later Cass's soldiers saw the Chippewa Indians raising the British flag in front of a wigwam. Cass ordered his 23 soldiers to get their guns. "Prepare for a possible fight," he warned.

Then Cass strode boldly into the Indian camp. He left his soldiers behind. Only his interpreter accompanied him. The interpreter could speak English and the Chippewa language. Cass said to the interpreter, "Tell the Indians no foreign flag can be raised over soil of the United States of America."

Cass reached out to the pole. He tore down the British flag and stepped on it. Boldly he took it back to his tent. As Cass walked away he knew his act might cause the Indians to attack.

But the Indians did not attack, thanks to the words of Neenay Johnston. She was

When Michigan was a territory, Governor Lewis Cass set out to prove that it was a good place to live. He and his men traveled 4,200 miles while exploring the territory.

respected by the Indian chiefs for three reasons. First, she was the daughter of an Indian chief. Second, she had gone to school. Third, she knew a lot about white people because she was married to a white man who lived at the Soo.

Neenay explained how foolish it would be to fight. If the Indians hurt Cass, the American nation would attack them.

The Indians took her advice. The chiefs agreed to meet the governor again. They told Cass he could build the fort. And they gave him the right to ten square miles along

John Johnston, who had served the British during the War of 1812, was the U.S. Indian agent at Sault Ste. Marie when Lewis Cass visited there in 1820.

the river. But the chiefs kept the right for Indians to set up their wigwams along the river and fish there.

Cass thanked them. He gave the chiefs blankets, knives, silverware, broadcloth and other goods.

Now Cass was ready to continue his trip around Michigan.

EARLY SURVEYS

Cass decided to take his trip because many people in the eastern states thought Michigan was a bad place to live.

That idea grew out of early surveys of the Michigan Territory. After the War of 1812 ended, the government sent men to survey the land in Michigan. The surveyors were supposed to divide the land into sections. Each section was to be one square mile in size. The sections or parts of them then could be sold to settlers.

Unfortunately the government sent the surveyors to Michigan during the wet season of a wet year—1815. When they came, Lewis Cass had been governor of the territory for only a short time.

After wading in mud and water and being soaked in rain, the surveyors stopped before they saw very much of Michigan. They had seen swamps, sandy soil and bogs. They said crops would not grow on the land and the climate would make people sick.

"The land is no good for farms or homes," the surveyors told the people back in the East. A popular poem said, "Don't go to Michigan, that land of ills; the word means ague, fever, and chills."

Cass, however, did not believe that Michigan was worthless. He decided to explore the territory himself and find out. He and his men left Detroit on May 25, 1820. He had carefully picked the people. They included a mapmaker, a geologist, a record keeper and others.

After his stormy meeting with the Indians at the Soo, Cass continued his trip. He went to Lake Superior and around the northern shoreline of the Upper Peninsula.

At that time Wisconsin was part of the Michigan Territory. So the Cass group went through Wisconsin to the upper part of the Mississippi River. They then moved south

LAKE SUPERIOR

SAULT STE. MARIE
(1820)

LA POINTE
(1842)

WASHINGTON
(1836)

CEDAR POINT
(1836)

LAKE HURON

WASHINGTON (1836)

SAGINAW
(1819)

LAKE MICHIGAN

DETROIT
(1807)

CHICAGO
(1821)

CAREY MISSION (1828)

CHICAGO (1833)   MAUMEE (1817)

GREENVILLE
(1795)

When the Indians and white men signed a treaty, it was a big event. The drawing above shows the scene of a treaty ceremony at Butte des Morts in 1827. Governor Lewis Cass of the Michigan Territory is in the boat. He and his men are arriving to meet with the Indians. At that time Butte des Morts was part of the Michigan Territory. (Later it became part of Wisconsin.) The map at left shows which lands were ceded by the eleven treaties that affected the area that eventually became the state of Michigan.

64

to Chicago. There they split into two groups. One came back to Detroit through southern Michigan. The other surveyed the western part of Michigan along the lake.

The 4,200-mile trip showed Cass and his men that Michigan might be a good place in which to live. It was more than a swamp. Soon after Cass and his men returned to Detroit, they wrote a report on their trip so that everyone could know more about Michigan. The report was published in the East. It helped give Michigan a better reputation in the East.

INDIAN TREATIES

Cass began to work out treaties with the Indians for more land for settlers. When Cass took over as governor of the territory, the white man had rights to only southeastern Michigan. The rest was Indian land.

Between 1817 and 1842 Cass and others signed nine treaties. The Indians ceded the rest of Michigan, except for some Indian reservations (lands kept for Indian use).

A typical Indian treaty was the Saginaw Treaty. In 1819 Cass asked the Ottawa and Chippewa Indians to meet him near where Saginaw now is. He had two ships sail from Detroit to Saginaw Bay filled with liquor, food and other gifts. The gifts would be given to the Indians when the treaty was signed.

A council house was built. Cass and his government people and the Indian chiefs met there for several weeks. During the treaty talks, several thousand Indians camped in the area.

Cass offered the Indians $3,000 in cash and a payment of $1,000 every year. Cass also said the government would have a blacksmith work for the Indians. In addition, the Indians would get farm tools. A teacher would show them how to use the tools.

In return the Indians would cede most of east-central Michigan to the whites.

But the Indians did not immediately sign the treaty. Soon Cass found out why. A white fur trapper named Jacob Smith opposed the treaty. He had lived with the Indians for years. They trusted and respected him. Because of Smith, they avoided signing.

Finally Cass solved the problem by giving Smith and his friends about 7,000 acres of land. The Indians then signed. And Cass ordered the opening of the whiskey that was on the ships.

Some payments promised to the Indians in the Michigan treaties were made. Some were not. And some hunting and fishing rights promised to the Indians were taken away later.

The white men had all the advantages in making treaties with the Indians. First, the white men had money to give, as well as liquor and food. Second, the Indians knew the white men had guns and more people. They might take the land if the Indians did not agree to cede it. Third, most Indians at that time had no schooling. They did not understand the legal and financial language Cass and others used. They also did not understand their own rights under civil law and treaty law. You can say the Indians were forced to give up their land.

Meanwhile the Indians lived here and there on pieces of land that new settlers had

After the Erie Canal (above) was completed in 1825, many immigrants settled in the Midwest. The canal ran through New York State. It allowed people to travel by water all the way from New York City to the Great Lakes. Michigan made great efforts to attract these settlers. Some Washtenaw County settlers wrote the advertisement at left. It tells about a society whose goal was to give information about Michigan to people looking for a new place to settle. (The words *emigrant* and *immigrant* have different meanings. An *emigrant* is someone leaving a place. An *immigrant* is someone coming to a place. The people leaving Europe thought of themselves as emigrants. People who were already in Michigan thought of them as immigrants.)

66

not yet bought. But the settlers in most places considered the Indians to be pests.

The white men in Michigan no longer needed the Indians to provide furs. Few furs were being trapped in Michigan by 1830. And there were fewer wild animals that the Indians could hunt for food. The Indians had none of the white men's money and little food. Life became difficult.

FORCING THE INDIANS WEST

Around 1830, the U.S. government tried to move all the Indians to the land west of the Mississippi River. Some people in the East and in the Great Lakes area just wanted to get rid of the Indians. Others, including Governor Cass, thought the Indians would be happier in the West because there were few white settlers there. Some said the Indians would have a better chance of preserving their culture in the West.

But most Indians wanted to stay in the area in which they and their ancestors had lived. One of those who was angry about moving was Chief Speckled Snake. In 1829, when his tribe was ordered to move, he told his people:

"Brothers! I have listened to many talks from our great father. When he first came over the wide waters, he was but a little man . . . very little. His legs were cramped by sitting long in his big boat. And he begged for a little land to light his fire on.

"But when the white man had warmed himself before the Indians' fire and filled himself with their hominy [corn meal], he became very large. With a step he bestrode the mountains, and his feet covered the plains and the valleys. His hands grasped

the eastern and western sea. And his head rested on the moon. Then he became our great father. He loved his red children, and he said, 'Get a little further, lest I tread on thee.'

"Brothers, I have listened to a great many talks from our great father. But they always began and ended in this—'Get a little further. You are too near to me.' "

Indians from all the states and territories were sent west. Michigan's Huron, or Wyandot, and some Potawatomi were sent to Kansas. A small number of Potawatomi won the right to stay in Michigan partly because they had bought land in Calhoun, Cass and Van Buren counties.

Meanwhile most of the Ottawa and Chippewa—who lived in the less settled northern part of the state—were allowed to stay in Michigan on reservations.

Today Indian reservations in Michigan cover only about 20,500 acres. The six federal reservations are (1) Bay Mills Indian Community near Brimley in Chippewa County, (2) the Hannahville Indian Community near Wilson in Menominee County, (3) the Keweenaw Bay Indian Community in Baraga County, (4) the Saginaw Chippewa Tribal Operations near Mt. Pleasant, (5) the Sault Ste. Marie Tribe of Chippewa at the Soo, and (6) the Grand Traverse Band of Ottawa and Chippewa Indians at Suttons Bay. Only 7,500 of 40,000 Michigan Indians now choose to live on these reservations.

GETTING PEOPLE TO MICHIGAN

Cass had told people about the good land in Michigan. He had made treaties with the

Indians so white settlers could claim the land. But transportation had to improve before many people would come.

One big improvement in transportation was the building of the Erie Canal in New York State. The canal was completed in 1825. It ran from the Hudson River in eastern New York State to Buffalo in the western part. People could ride barges pulled by mules to Buffalo. Then they could transfer to Great Lakes steamboats to go to Detroit and other Great Lakes ports. Now people from New England, New York and other eastern states began to come to Michigan by water. They did not have to travel on rough roads for many days. Also, the things they produced in Michigan could now be shipped to the East at a much lower cost.

MICHIGAN ROADS

Once settlers arrived in Michigan, roads were still a problem. The roads used at first were not roads at all. They were rough Indian trails. Bridges existed only in the Detroit area. Elsewhere settlers had to wade across river and streams.

The southern part of the state was settled first. As men worked their way west from Detroit, they blazed the trail by cutting marks in trees along the way. This helped them find their way back to buy tools, farm animals or food. It also helped pioneers who followed.

The first roads built by white men were for the army. General Hull built one south from Detroit to Monroe during the War of 1812. But it was not used much after the war, and the forest soon covered it up. In 1818 the government began to repair and widen it. The government also began to build bridges over streams.

That same year, 1818, the U.S. government sent troops to build a military road north from Detroit toward Pontiac. A military road was used by everybody, but it was built especially so soldiers and equipment could move from one important place to another. This road cost $1,000 a mile to build. That was a great price in those days.

The Pontiac road building slowed down when the workers came to a swamp called Cranberry Marsh. To cross the swamp, the soldiers made frames of logs. They pushed these deep into the swamp. On these they laid more logs, other timber, brush, clay and sand to make a dry highway.

Governor Cass asked the federal government for two other military roads. One would go from Detroit to Port Huron. The other would run from Detroit to Chicago. Both took many years to plan and build. The roads helped to shorten travel time. For instance, the southern road cut the trip from Detroit to Ypsilanti from four days to one day.

In wet places, road builders laid logs side by side across the road. They called these corduroy roads. Like corduroy material, they were bumpy. Wagons often got stuck while traveling over them. When this happened, people earned money by getting the wagons out of the mud.

If a coach or cart did not break down, that was good luck. With good luck it might take only a week to travel 100 miles or so. With bad luck, it took twice that long. With fair luck, a pioneer family traveled ten miles a day.

As roads got better, many people traveled by stagecoach. Each trip still took a long time. The coach stopped for meals and overnight rest at inns like this one. A Detroit to Chicago trip took four and one-half days.

THE UPPER PENINSULA

It was a long time before the Upper Peninsula had any roads. In the fur-trading days, between about 1700 and 1830, the people had not needed roads. They traveled on the lakes and rivers.

Fur trading declined in the Upper Peninsula in the 1830s. Within ten years the search for copper and iron replaced the search for furs. The only roads connected the mines with shipping docks. At that time people valued the Upper Peninsula for its natural resources and not for settlement.

GOING BY WATER

In pioneer days it was much easier to travel by water than by land.

Until 1818 all the ships coming to Michigan were powered by sails. Then the first steamboat, the *Walk-in-the-Water*, appeared. People were surprised. Indians suggested the ship was being pulled by a giant sturgeon; the Great Lakes' largest fish.

The *Walk-in-the-Water* had two steam-powered paddle wheels. She also had two masts that could carry sails. The ship had a smokestack 30 feet high. She carried 40 cords of wood to burn to make her engine run and 20 paying passengers.

Since the steam whistle had not been invented, a small cannon stood on deck. The crew fired it to tell people the *Walk-in-the-Water* was coming into port.

The *Walk-in-the-Water* used its sails in fair weather. She moved almost twice as fast as with the engine alone. But she did not have to stand still, like a sailboat, when the breeze stopped blowing.

In 1818 the Walk-in-the-Water *became the first steamship on the Great Lakes. It also used sails for power and fired a small cannon to announce that it was coming into port. It ran aground in 1821 and its passengers had to be rescued.*

The *Michigan,* built in 1833, was the first large cabin steamer constructed in Detroit. She had 48 berths (built-in beds) for men and 60 for women and children. Six years later the *Great Western* appeared with the first upper cabins built above the main deck. This gave her 60 more staterooms (180 more berths) than had been possible before. Ship travel was becoming pleasant!

Shipyards for building sailboats and wooden steamships were started in Michigan. Boats were made of oak, chestnut and pine, which grew nearby. The first shipyards were in Detroit and Monroe. Later, yards were opened in St. Clair, Port Huron, East Saginaw and Bay City.

All early shipyards looked much alike. Each had its own lumber mill. There was a dry dock, where the boat was put together. Hulls of old ships were often used as dry docks for new hulls. It took a long time to build a sturdy boat.

THE FIRST RAILROADS

In the 1840s, railroads began to carry settlers to Michigan. The first railroad built west of New York State was opened in Michigan in 1836. It ran from Adrian to Toledo on Lake Erie. It was called the Erie and Kalamazoo Railroad, but it never ran beyond Adrian. The first year horses pulled the railroad cars along the rails. The next year the Erie and Kalamazoo began operating Michigan's first steam locomotive.

At about the same time, the state decided to build three state-owned railroads. All would run from east to west. At the southern edge of the state, one would go from Monroe to New Buffalo. A little farther north, one would run from Detroit to St. Joseph. Even farther north, the third would run from Port Huron to Grand Rapids.

The state did not have enough money to complete all the lines. One ran from Monroe to Hillsdale and another from Detroit to

In 1837 Michigan's first railroad, the Erie and Kalamazoo, looked something like this. It ran from Toledo, Ohio, to Adrian. When the railroad began in 1836, horses instead of a steam locomotive pulled the cars along the rails.

Kalamazoo. In 1846 the state sold these two southern railroads to private firms.

By 1852 two private Michigan railroads had reached Chicago. Others were also doing well. Later, private firms got financial help from several places. First, the federal government gave land free to railroads. The railroads could sell their land to pay for new tracks and equipment. Second, railroads paid one small railroad tax, but they did not pay other state or local taxes. Third, people in towns and villages wanted to encourage railroads to come through their areas. So they offered railroads money to help pay for construction.

The coming of the railroads in the 1830s and 1840s was as great a change as the coming of the airplane in the twentieth century. Before the railroad came, it took a horse-drawn wagon anywhere from a day to a day and a half to go from Ann Arbor to Detroit. When the Michigan Central Railroad began operating in 1839, the train covered the same 38 miles in only two and a half hours.

CONCLUSION

Between 1820 and 1850 many things happened that made Michigan more attractive to settlers.

1. Governor Cass explored the Michigan Territory and found out that it had good land for farming. He let people in the East know this.
2. Cass and others arranged treaties with Michigan's various Indian tribes so that white settlers could buy land.
3. Travel became easier with the building of the Erie Canal, better roads, steamships and railroads.

In the next chapter, we will talk about the settlers who came to Michigan because of these changes and about how they formed a new state.

THE NEXT STORY

In this chapter the Michigan Territory becomes the nation's twenty-sixth state. The people who govern the new state organize a school system, improve transportation and choose a new state capital.

PEOPLE

Stevens T. Mason was the first governor of the state of Michigan.

Isaac Crary, a Marshall lawyer, led the effort to design a good public school system for Michigan.

John Pierce, a Marshall minister and Crary's friend, was the first head of Michigan's public school system.

Lucinda Stone believed that women should be able to go to college.

PLACES

Marshall was one of many towns that hoped to become the state capital.

Lansing was a wilderness area with only a few settlers when the legislature selected it as the state capital in 1847.

The Upper Peninsula's first plank road ran from **Marquette** to **Negaunee** and **Ishpeming**.

WORDS

A **census** is an official count of the number of people living in an area.

A **constitution** lists the basic principles or rules for running a government.

The **Toledo Strip** was the land south of what is now Michigan. It was claimed by both Michigan and Ohio before Michigan became a state.

The **Northwest Ordinance** was a United States law passed in 1787. It told how territories could become states.

The **Land Ordinance of 1785** was a United States law that told how land was to be divided into plots for sale to settlers. It set aside some of the land to be used to raise funds for public schools.

WHEN DID IT HAPPEN?

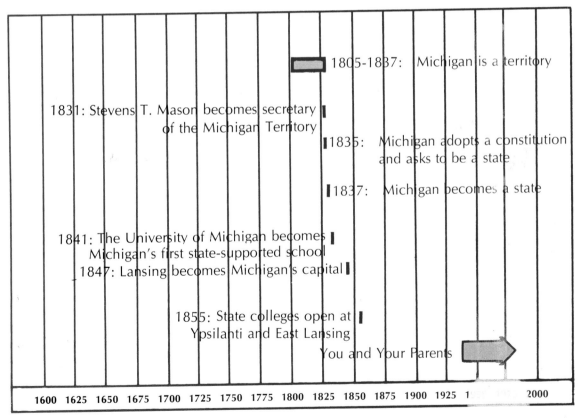

1805-1837: Michigan is a territory

1831: Stevens T. Mason becomes secretary of the Michigan Territory

1835: Michigan adopts a constitution and asks to be a state

1837: Michigan becomes a state

1841: The University of Michigan becomes Michigan's first state-supported school

1847: Lansing becomes Michigan's capital

1855: State colleges open at Ypsilanti and East Lansing

You and Your Parents

1600 1625 1650 1675 1700 1725 1750 1775 1800 1825 1850 1875 1900 1925 1   2000

CHAPTER SIX
MICHIGAN BECOMES A STATE

In the White House one day in 1831, President Andrew Jackson was talking to two visitors, John Mason, of Michigan, and John's young son, Stevens.

John was secretary of the growing Michigan Territory. As secretary, he was the governor's main assistant. He became acting governor when the governor was out of the territory. However, John wanted to go to Texas, so he told the president that he wanted to resign.

John then asked the president to appoint his son, Stevens T. Mason, as the new secretary. Stevens had helped his father with his work as secretary, and he knew a lot about Michigan.

The president knew that Stevens was only 19 years old. He also knew that Lewis Cass was about to resign as territorial governor to become the United States secretary of war. When that happened, the new Michigan secretary would be the acting governor. However, President Jackson was impressed with both John Mason's plea and Stevens Mason's experience. He agreed to make Stevens the new secretary.

When the news of Stevens T. Mason's appointment reached Michigan, some people were upset. They said Stevens was a minor—someone not old enough to vote. They did not want to be governed by someone who could not vote. In Detroit, 162 people signed a paper asking the president to remove Stevens from office.

Immediately Stevens wrote a long letter to President Jackson. He said that the people who did not like him were Jackson's political enemies and asked for the president's support. He also published a letter "To the Public" in a Detroit newspaper. In it he promised to listen to the advice of older men.

Susan
Price

Stevens T. Mason was one of the youngest men ever to act as governor of a territory. When Michigan held its first state election in 1835, he was selected as governor.

At the age of 19, Stevens Mason was appointed secretary of the Michigan Territory. Here he is sworn in. Territorial Chief Justice William Woodbridge is holding the Bible and Territorial Governor Lewis Cass is giving the oath. Mason's father is at the far right.

President Jackson decided to keep Stevens in office. He soon appointed George Porter to replace Cass as governor. Porter often was gone from the territory. When he was absent, Mason served as acting governor. Mason's experience in handling the job of governor was important. In 1834, Porter died. Stevens was only 22 years old, but President Jackson decided to let him continue to serve as acting governor.

MICHIGAN WANTS TO BE A STATE

The Michigan Territory was growing fast. Many wanted it to become a state. People in a state could elect their governor instead of having the president appoint him. Their representatives could vote in the United States Congress.

Already Michigan's neighbors to the south—Ohio, Indiana and Illinois—had become states. Stevens T. Mason became one of the leaders of the drive to make Michigan a state.

To become a state, Michigan had to prove that 60,000 people lived within its boundaries. Governor Mason ordered that the people be counted. This counting, or census, showed that more than 85,000 people lived in the Lower Peninsula alone.

The Michigan Constitution of 1835 was placed in a metal can and forgotten for many years. Later someone looking through some old junk at the capitol found the can. The tattered constitution was carefully restored and is now in the State Archives.

WRITING A CONSTITUTION

The next step was to write a state constitution. A constitution is different from a law. It sets up the basic rules for governing the state. All laws passed by the legislature must conform to the constitution's basic principles.

In Michigan, on April 4, 1835, the people elected 91 representatives to write their constitution. When the constitution was finished, the people would vote again on whether or not to accept it.

The people who wrote the constitution began with a list of rights much like the Bill of Rights in the national Constitution. They included things like freedom to worship.

Next came a description of the government of the new state. There would be a house of representatives with 48 to 100 members and a smaller senate. Representatives would be elected every year. Senators, the governor and the lieutenant governor would have two-year terms. Judges would be appointed.

One of the hardest things to decide was who could vote in elections. In some states you had to own property to vote. But Michigan decided every white man over 21

Elections were exciting events in the 1830s. This painting by T.H.O.P. Burnham shows Michigan's first election after becoming a state. Stevens T. Mason, who was reelected governor, is in front wearing a tall black hat. The Detroit City Hall is on the right.

years old could vote if he had lived in the state for six months. Women, Indians and blacks were not allowed to vote.

The most unusual part of the constitution was the section on education. It made the state instead of local groups responsible for education. This meant schools would be more alike in their programs and in the amount of money they had to spend.

On October 5, 1835, the voters of Michigan accepted this constitution. They also elected Stevens T. Mason as governor.

Michigan was now ready for statehood. But it needed the approval of the United States Congress in Washington, D.C. There was a problem. The problem was the boundary between Ohio and Michigan. The struggle over this problem is known as the Toledo War.

Both Ohio and Michigan claimed the land called the Toledo Strip. Both Ohio and Michigan sent armed men there. These men acted like they wanted to fight. But no shots were fired. Only one man was even injured. Some say that during this time Ohio people started calling Michiganians "Wolverines." Wolverines were known as very vicious, bad animals.

In the Toledo War, Michigan claimed the border was the bottom dotted line. Ohio claimed the upper dotted line. Congress settled on the black line. In return, Congress gave Michigan the part of the Upper Peninsula shown in red.

western Upper Peninsula

Toledo Strip

MICHIGAN'S UPPER PENINSULA

In the U.S. Congress, Ohio legislators argued for their boundary. Michigan was still a territory, so its representatives could listen to the arguments, but they could not speak in Congress. Also, the president did not want people in Ohio to be angry with him because an election was coming up. Finally Congress decided the Toledo Strip would be part of Ohio.

In place of Toledo, Congress gave Michigan a lot of land in the western part of the Upper Peninsula. Before that, only the land around St. Ignace and Sault Ste. Marie had belonged to Michigan.

At first many in Michigan did not want to trade Ohio land for U.P. land. To them, the Upper Peninsula was only a wilderness. They knew Toledo was a good port on Lake Erie. They did not know about the copper, iron ore and timber that would make the Upper Peninsula such a valuable part of Michigan.

Finally, Michigan gave up its claim to the Toledo Strip. And in 1837 the U.S. Congress made Michigan the twenty-sixth state. The new state government had many things to decide. It needed to organize a school system, find a permanent place for a state capital and improve transportation.

In Michigan's early years, most schools were made of logs. Children from all ages went to school in the same room. They got their water from a pump outside the school instead of a drinking fountain.

BUILDING SCHOOLS

When Michigan was a territory, it had no school program. Some groups of people in towns set up schools, but very few children went to school. Many did not live near a school, and many spent their time helping their parents at home.

The people who wrote Michigan's first constitution thought schools were important. The school system they created was based on an old federal law and some new state laws.

The federal law was the Land Ordinance of 1785. It set up the system for selling land in Michigan and other territories to settlers. It divided the land into townships that were six miles wide and six miles long. It set aside one square mile of land, called a section, in each township for education. When the school section was sold, the income was used for public schools.

In most places the school land went to the townships. But when Michigan became a state, it convinced the U.S. Congress to give the school land to the state. The state

got enough money from the wise sale of this land to build a good school system. Any township that wanted a school could have money from the state fund if it followed certain rules and had a school tax. The state money was divided up according to the number of students in each school.

Under its new constitution, Michigan was the first state to have a state head of education. He was called the superintendent of public instruction. He set up a system of public education that included primary schools and a state university. He managed the education money and set standards for schools to meet.

The first public schools were often log buildings. Each building usually had only one room. Students from age 5 to age 17 sat in the room together. The teacher worked with a small group of students while the others studied at their desks. Older children often helped younger ones. Some Michigan log one-room schools were still being used in 1900. A few children in Michigan attend one-room schools today.

As a new state, Michigan became a national leader in public education. Isaac Crary (left) and John Pierce (right) planned most of Michigan's education system. Both were from Marshall. Pierce also became Michigan's first superintendent of public instruction.

In 1887, people wanted to have men for teachers. They thought men could control the older boys better. Sometimes teachers used a switch, a leather strap or a paddle to punish children who misbehaved.

Two men from Marshall—a lawyer, Isaac Crary, and a minister, John Pierce—planned most of Michigan's education system. Crary was among those elected to draw up the constitution. He wrote the part dealing with education. Governor Mason asked Crary who would be a good superintendent of public instruction. Crary suggested Pierce.

The first thing Pierce did was to see how states in the East ran their education systems. The new state did not have money to pay for his trip, so he paid his own way. He came back to Michigan with the firm belief that:

1. Primary school students should not pay for their education.
2. All children should be required to go to school.
3. Teachers should have special training and be paid a minimum wage.

Many years would pass before all of these ideas became part of Michigan's education system. It was not until 1869, for example, that the state said that no public primary school could charge tuition fees.

The first Michigan law on education created the primary schools and the University of Michigan.

The one-room school was common in rural Michigan well after 1900. There were no school buses then, so students had to attend schools close to their homes. Students had to help with school chores such as bringing in wood for the stove. In the state's early years, the teachers in most schools were men. People thought that men teachers could do a better job of controlling boys than women teachers could. Also, women were not encouraged to go to school long enough to become teachers.

People in Michigan believed that higher education was important. These pictures show how some of the state's early campuses looked. From the top are Albion College, the University of Michigan and Michigan Agricultural College (now Michigan State University).

Lucinda Stone of Kalamazoo was a leader in efforts to gain rights for women.

MICHIGAN'S UNIVERSITIES

In 1837, almost all higher education in the nation was provided by colleges set up by churches. There were a few state universities, but most were not doing well. Michigan decided to set up the University of Michigan and build it in Ann Arbor. In 1841 the new school opened its doors. By 1867, it was the largest university in the nation, with 1,255 students. Crary and Pierce thought higher education should provide several things:

1. Courses in agriculture,
2. Teacher training programs, and
3. Classes for women.

In 1855 the state legislature created Michigan Agricultural College. At that time there were no state agricultural colleges in the United States.

Seven years later, the college received a grant of 240,000 acres of land from the U.S. Congress. The land could be used or sold to finance the college. Thus Michigan Agricultural College became the nation's oldest "land grant" college. Today it teaches many subjects besides agriculture and is called Michigan State University.

Michigan was also the first western state to have a state teachers' college. The college, opened in 1852 at Ypsilanti, is now known as Eastern Michigan University.

During this time, a number of churches started private colleges in Michigan. The first was Kalamazoo College, founded in 1836 by the Baptists. Four other early private colleges were Albion (Methodist), Olivet (Congregational), Adrian (Methodist) and Hillsdale (Baptist).

THE FIRST COEDS

In the early nineteenth century, only men went to college. Men were the only people allowed to vote, and they held virtually all the government and business jobs.

Most women did housework, raised children and helped with farm work. But some women did not want to marry and manage households. Others wanted jobs like those done by their fathers and brothers at least until they married. Still others simply enjoyed learning enough to want to continue school after public school. In 1851 Michigan Central College in Spring Arbor (near Jackson) became the first Michigan college to grant a degree to a woman. The college, which later became Hillsdale College, was only the second one in the United States to admit women. From its beginning in 1852,

When Michigan was a territory, its capitol (left) was located in Detroit. After Michigan became a state, the capital remained Detroit for a while. Then, in 1847, the state legislature voted to make Lansing Michigan's capital city. Very few people lived in Lansing then. The painting above shows construction of the first Lansing capitol, a wooden building.

In 1872 Michigan laid the cornerstone for a new capitol. Finished in 1879, the limestone building is still our capitol.

Eastern Michigan, then known as Michigan Normal, admitted men and women.

A leader in gaining rights and opportunities for women was Lucinda Stone of Kalamazoo. She headed the women's part of Kalamazoo College. And she led the drive that opened the University of Michigan to women in 1870. That same year, Michigan State University, then Michigan Agricultural College, also began to admit women.

CHOOSING A NEW CAPITAL CITY

During the years when Michigan was a territory, its capitol building was in Detroit. However, the 1835 constitution said the legislature should select a new capital site.

In 1847 the legislature began discussing where to put a permanent capitol building. J. Wright Gordon of Marshall was governor. He believed his home town should be the capital. He built a new home there and told some people it would be the governor's mansion.

In the legislature, many places were suggested as a capital city—Marshall, Detroit, Ann Arbor, Charlotte, Battle Creek, Jackson, Ionia, Owosso, Howell, Pontiac, Caledonia and Lyons.

Detroit was opposed by some because it was too close to Canada. In a war, it could be attacked easily. Ann Arbor was opposed by some because it already had the university. Jackson was opposed because it already had the prison. Marshall was opposed by those who wanted the capital located farther north, more in the center of the Lower Peninsula.

Then a landowner named James Seymour offered to give the state twenty acres in Ingham County for the capital. The area did not even have a name. At first it was called "Michigan." It was a wilderness. No roads, railroads or stage coaches came near it. But "Michigan" won in the final vote. It was named Lansing.

The new state capitol was a white frame building. It opened in 1848. Soon the new building was too small. But it was used for thirty years before the present capitol building was built.

Michigan's early dirt roads were poor. Wheels stuck in the mud and soft earth. So people began to build plank roads. The companies that built the roads put up toll gates about every 10 miles so that they could charge travelers for using the roads.

THE PLANK ROADS

To get to Lansing and other places in Michigan, people rode wagons and stagecoaches on dirt roads. Often these vehicles got stuck in mud. The new state needed better roads. The solution was to build plank roads. Long boards were laid parallel to the road. Then thick, wide wooden planks were placed across the boards.

When the Howell to Lansing road opened in 1852, it was a treat to see the four-horse stagecoach moving through each town. The driver blew a tin horn as he came into town. People gathered around the stage stop to see who was traveling and to hear news from other towns. In 1853 the Upper Peninsula got its first plank road. It ran from Marquette on the shore of Lake Superior to the iron mines in Negaunee and Ishpeming.

Private companies built other plank roads. The companies put up toll gates about every 10 miles and made travelers pay to use the roads. Under state law, travelers could be charged:

1. Two cents per mile for a wagon and two animals.
2. One cent per mile for a wagon and one animal.
3. One cent per mile for a horse and rider.
4. Two cents per mile for every 20 sheep or hogs.

Plank roads were a great improvement. Trips that took from 4 to 6 days on dirt roads could be made in 10 to 14 hours on plank roads. The roads were noisy too. Another problem was that the planks rotted and had to often be replaced. The state legislature gave companies permission to build 5,082 miles of plank roads, but the companies finished only 1,179 miles of them.

CONCLUSION

Michigan decided it wanted to be a state in 1835. It wrote a constitution that allowed all white men to vote and it set up an unusual educational system.

Before Michigan became a state, it had to settle an argument with Ohio over the Toledo Strip. Michigan lost the Toledo Strip, but it gained the western Upper Peninsula. Michigan became a state on January 26, 1837. The state's first governor was Stevens T. Mason.

The new state set up public primary schools and a university. It would be a leader in education for many years.

In 1848, the new capitol opened in Lansing. To improve transportation to Lansing and other places, people built plank roads.

In the next chapter, we will visit some of the pioneer settlers who lived in Michigan during its first years of statehood.

Mackinac Island

Beaver Island

Lansing

Yankee Springs

THE NEXT STORY

As this chapter starts, thousands of new settlers are coming to Michigan. Most of them buy land that will be used for farming. Pioneer life is difficult, but these people are determined to succeed.

PEOPLE

William Lewis brought his family from New York State by barge over the Erie Canal and settled in western Michigan.

Mary Lewis was William's young daughter.

James Strang led a Mormon group that settled in Michigan.

William Beaumont made important discoveries about the stomach while taking care of **Alexis St. Martin** on Mackinac Island.

PLACES

Yankee Springs was a small community in Barry County. The Lewis family lived there.

Beaver Island, in northern Lake Michigan, was where James Strang's Mormon group settled.

90

WORDS

An **almanac** is a book of facts and ideas about many things. It is published once each year.

A **pioneer** is someone who does something other people have not done. This chapter's pioneers settle new land and discover things about medicine.

A **frontier** is an area where few people live or one that people do not know a lot about. For example, in the 1820s Ohio had many settlers and Michigan was the frontier. Today outer space is a frontier.

An **immigrant** is a person who moves to a new country.

WHEN DID IT HAPPEN?

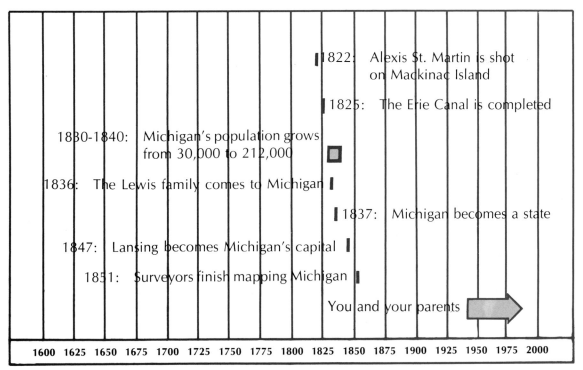

1822:   Alexis St. Martin is shot on Mackinac Island

1825:   The Erie Canal is completed

1830-1840:   Michigan's population grows from 30,000 to 212,000

1836:   The Lewis family comes to Michigan

1837:   Michigan becomes a state

1847:   Lansing becomes Michigan's capital

1851:   Surveyors finish mapping Michigan

You and your parents

1600 1625 1650 1675 1700 1725 1750 1775 1800 1825 1850 1875 1900 1925 1950 1975 2000

CHAPTER SEVEN MICHIGAN'S PIONEER SETTLERS

In 1836 Mary Lewis was one of five children who came to Michigan with their mother and father. She and her family lived in Barry County, halfway between the present cities of Grand Rapids and Battle Creek.

One day Mary went for a ride on her pony. She had learned how to ride when she was very young. She rode alone. Only a few other settlers lived in Barry County then. She enjoyed having nature's birds and trees as her neighbors as she bounced along on her pony.

She guided her pony two and one-half miles through the forest. It was farther than Mary had ever ridden. As she moved through a cluster of trees, she saw a beautiful lake that she had not seen before.

Mary gazed at the broad sheet of water. In it she saw a perfect reflection of the trees. When she was older, Mary wrote about seeing Gun Lake.

"As I silently gazed, a feeling of awe stole over me. The solemn stillness of the lake and forest frightened me. I turned my pony and fled. I never drew rein until my home was reached."

Mary was 4 years old when she and her family moved to Michigan from New York State. As pioneers, the Lewis family had to work hard. They had to make many sacrifices.

The first thing Mary's father did was to build a cabin. He cut down trees. Then neighbors helped him notch the logs so they could be fitted together at the corners of the house. Together the men raised the logs to form the walls. A door and window were sawed out after the walls were in place. Then the men added a roof made from wooden shingles.

Mary did not notice the hardships or loneliness of pioneer life. She spent a lot of time with her father. She rode with him by wagon or on horseback to all the neighbors' houses. She even traveled on the stagecoach with him.

The Lewis family was among the thousands who settled in Michigan between 1830 and 1840. In those ten years Michigan grew faster than any other state or territory. There were at least two reasons Michigan grew so fast: the Erie Canal and Michigan's cheap land.

THE ERIE CANAL

When Mr. and Mrs. Lewis decided to move from New York State, they had to sell or give away most of their belongings. They only had room for the boxes and trunks they could load onto one wagon.

Mary's father drove their wagon to the canal. The children rode in the back of the wagon, and Mrs. Lewis followed on a saddle horse. At the canal, the Lewis family joined other pioneers from New England

William Lewis was Mary's father. They were among the thousands of New Yorkers who came to Michigan in the 1830s.

and New York. The wagon was towed aboard a barge. Then the wheels were removed. That kept the wagon from rolling around. The canal barge took the Lewis family to Lake Erie. They then took a steamship to Michigan.

AVAILABLE FARM LAND

Michigan grew because the Erie Canal made travel to Michigan easier. It also grew because the government was selling land for only $1.25 an acre. An acre is nearly as large as a football field. Mary's father bought one thousand acres in 1836.

That year the government sold more land in Michigan than in any other state or territory. It sold land worth more than $5.25 million. That was one-fifth of all the money

Surveyors mapped the wilderness. By 1840, all of the Lower Peninsula was surveyed. The Upper Peninsula was finished in 1851. The surveyors also learned much about Michigan's resources. For example, one of them discovered much of the iron in the Upper Peninsula.

the government made from land sales that year. The government had sales offices in Detroit, Monroe, White Pigeon, Kalamazoo, Flint, Ionia and East Saginaw. At times men stood in line to buy land. Often two men raced to the land office because they both wanted the same land.

People like Mary's father knew exactly what land they were buying because the land had been carefully surveyed. The surveyors went into the wilderness to mark off townships, map the area and record what kind of land was there. By 1840 all of the Lower Peninsula had been surveyed. Surveyors finished their work in the Upper Peninsula in 1851.

People like William Lewis were pioneers in two ways. They lived on the frontier of settlement where few other people lived. They were also on the frontier of learning how to farm Michigan's land. During the French and British periods, most white men in Michigan had been fur traders. But by the 1830s fur trading in Michigan was dying out. Too many of the fur-bearing animals had been shot or trapped.

Most Michigan farming in those early days had been done near the forts at Detroit and Mackinac. By the time the Lewis family came in 1836, farms were scattered all over Michigan's southern counties.

Throughout Michigan, the population was booming. It went from 30,000 in 1830 to 212,000 in 1840. No other state or territory in the United States grew that fast during those years.

Settlers came to Michigan for many reasons. Blacks came to escape slavery. William Allen (left) farmed in Cass County. Elizabeth Forth (right) lived in Detroit.

James Jesse Strang (left) established a Mormon settlement on Beaver Island in 1847. That same year Albertus Van Raalte (right) founded the Holland Colony in western Michigan.

96

SETTLERS CAME FROM MANY PLACES

As the state moved through the 1840s and 1850s, people moved to Michigan for various reasons. Most thought Michigan would be a better place to live than their old homes. Some, like the Lewis family, came from other parts of the United States. Others immigrated to Michigan from foreign countries.

Many people from Ireland came to Michigan because of the 1840s potato famine. There was not enough food in Ireland to feed everyone.

Sometimes those who came from the same place settled together in the same rural community. For example, the Dutch settled along the coast of Lake Michigan. They named two of their towns Holland and Zeeland. (Zeeland is a province in the Netherlands.)

You can still see some of the ideas and ways of doing things that the immigrants brought to Michigan. For instance, fences made from tree stumps are still found in Montcalm County, northeast of Grand Rapids. Immigrants from Denmark began building fences this way in the 1850s.

Michigan invited immigrants to settle on its land. For example, Germans were good farmers. So Michigan sent a man to New York City to meet ships from Europe. He gave out handbooks about Michigan, printed in both German and English. That is one reason so many Germans came to Michigan.

Blacks were also among the early settlers in Michigan. Some had been slaves of British and French settlers. Many were free blacks who were part of the wave of settlers from New England and New York. Others had been slaves in southern states. Some had been freed by their masters, and others had run away from their owners.

People who believed in the Quaker religion began helping fugitive slaves settle in Cass County in 1836. In 1849, John Saunders, a Virginian, freed all of his slaves and bought land for them in Cass. As more free and escaping blacks moved to Cass, they built churches and schools. Some were farmers, some chose other professions, and some held public office. By the 1860 U.S. Census 1,356 blacks lived in Cass County. Only Wayne County had more black residents than Cass.

THE MORMONS AT BEAVER ISLAND

Some groups of settlers came to Michigan because they thought they could change, or reform, society. They had strict rules and often tried to keep other people away from their communities.

One especially unusual settlement in Michigan involved a Mormon religious group. They had strict beliefs against drinking and swearing. But they also believed a man could have more than one wife at a time. This is called polygamy. Because many non-Mormons believed that polygamy should not be tolerated, the Mormons tried to live together in places that had few other settlers.

In 1847 James Jesse Strang brought his Mormon group to Beaver Island in Lake Michigan. The best-known Mormon group settled in Salt Lake City, Utah. There are many Mormons in the United States today, but they no longer practice polygamy.

Well beyond the 1830s, Michigan settlers used wood from the forests around them to build their homes. This photo was taken near Traverse City around 1860.

The Mormons on Beaver Island dominated that part of the Lower Peninsula. Their members were elected to government jobs, and Strang served two terms in the Michigan legislature. Strang also had himself crowned king.

Mormon customs, especially polygamy, angered the Irish fishermen who lived near Beaver Island. The two groups often fought. On June 16, 1856, two men shot Strang. He died about three weeks later. After Strang died, people from the mainland sailed to Beaver Island. They forced most of the Mormons to leave. They also took or destroyed all of the Mormons' belongings.

PIONEER LIFE

Settlers like the Lewis family at Gun Lake produced most of their own food. If they had eggs, it was because they had chickens. If they had milk, it was because they had a cow or a goat. If they had corn, it was because they grew it. If they had meat, it was because they hunted.

Often they ran out of things they could not grow, such as sugar or tea. That meant a long walk or a long horseback ride to the nearest village with a store.

The winter season was always the hardest. By the end of the winter, a family might have only cornmeal left to eat. That meant

One popular form of frontier entertainment was barn raisings. Friends, relatives and neighbors all helped construct the barn. Often a whole barn could be built in only one day.

cornmeal mush for breakfast, for lunch and for dinner. Imagine no fruit, or vegetables.

In those years, small villages did not have clothing stores. Most pioneers did not have money to spend on clothes. Women made clothes by hand.

But pioneer life was not all hard work. There were special fun days, too. Mary Lewis remembered Thanksgiving, 1838. Her father invited all the settlers from miles around to the Lewis house. Their Indian neighbors brought wild turkeys and cranberries. Mary's mother made mince and pumpkin pies. After dinner, it began to snow. The harder it snowed, the livelier the

party grew. An old violin was pulled out, and everyone began dancing. They kept it up until morning. Then they ate breakfast and returned home.

EARLY FARMING

Some settlers thought prairie land was the best for farming. No trees had to be cut down. Prairies in southern Michigan were small—only a mile or two across. The soil under the thick prairie grass was very rich. But the thick grass made it hard to plow the land.

Other settlers chose oak openings. Here the oak trees stood far apart. No other trees or bushes grew in their shade. The pioneers had to cut down some of the trees, but it was easier to plow the land.

Farming was hard work. Men, women and children worked from the time the sun came up until it set. They could plow only about one acre a day. A heavy plow needed six oxen and two men to guide the oxen. A boy, following behind the plow, broke up the clods of earth.

Most pioneers brought an iron plow blade from the East. After settling on their land, they built a plow handle from wood. Where the roots of the grass went very deep, the regular plow could not do the work. So a man with a special, stronger plow was hired. The second plowing was always much easier than the first.

The weather was often a problem. Late frosts or heavy rains could delay spring planting. If too much rain fell in the autumn, a farmer could not harvest his crops. Floods drove many pioneers out of their cabins. Lightning sometimes killed cattle.

If the summers were too dry, the corn did not grow. The ears dried before they were ripe. The wheat turned brown and fell to the ground before it could be cut.

At first farmers planted the crops they had grown in New York and New England—especially potatoes, corn and beans. Later they learned· what crops grew best in Michigan.

FARMING EXPANDS

As transportation improved, the settlers began to sell some of their farm products in other states. Wheat, wool, fruit, chickens, pigs and cattle were all sent east. By 1850

Almanacs gave farmers advice on when to plant and harvest their crops. Horses or oxen pulled the machines the farmers used.

Michigan was the nation's fourth largest producer of wool and ninth largest grower of wheat.

Some farmers drained swampland and grew cranberries, peppermint and celery. Along the west shore of Michigan, the fruit industry developed. Lake Michigan warmed the winds that blew over a strip about 40 miles wide along the coast. Here apples, peaches, plums and cherries grew.

After 1860 horse-drawn corn planters and threshing machines made farming easier. Later, steam-driven machines helped the farmers even more.

100

In 1889, when this photo was taken, many Michigan farmers still lived in log homes. This Antrim County family grew their own vegetables. Many farmers would read an almanac to get tips on vegetable gardening. They hoped to avoid frosts in the spring months and dry spells in the summer months. The almanac predicted what weather to expect. Unfortunately the almanac was often wrong.

THE ALMANAC

Pioneer families sometimes relied on an almanac for advice. This little book told them what to do for sickness and many other things. Though often wrong, it predicted what weather to expect. It also told them the best time to plant their crops. Advice was given in rhymes like this:

An evening red and a morning grey
Will set the traveler on his way,
But an evening grey and a morning red
Will pour down rain on the pilgrim's head.

Pioneers planted seeds as early as they could. Of corn, their almanacs said:

Put me in in May
And I'll come right away.

A good corn crop would be:

Knee high
By the fourth of July.

These rules were for turnips:

Seventeenth of July
Plant your turnips, wet or dry
Harvest them the twelfth October
Drunk or sober.

Cabbages were to be planted at apple blossom time, when the moon was new, or at four o'clock in the morning.

This 1844 painting shows the tavern that William Lewis, Mary's father, built. The tavern was the stagecoach stop at Yankee Springs. As many as one hundred travelers could sleep there overnight. The stables could hold sixty teams of horses.

ROADS AND TAVERNS

In early Michigan, taverns did the same job as motels do today. Travelers left their horses in the tavern's stables and ate and slept in the tavern. Taverns were needed because the rutted, swampy roads made travel slow. Too few bridges also slowed travel. A wagon could go only ten or twenty miles a day.

The first roads followed old Indian trails. They were widened to handle wagons. The Chicago Road, now US-12 in southern Michigan, was probably the busiest road in the territory in the 1830s. Many settlers also used the Territorial Road, which today is Interstate 94.

Mary Lewis's father owned a tavern. Most of the people who stopped there were traveling between Battle Creek and Grand Rapids. As business grew, Mr. Lewis built extra wooden buildings where people could sleep. Eventually he added six buildings to his house. Some nights as many as one hundred people slept there. Sixty teams of horses might be in the Lewis stables at one time.

This stagecoach, photographed at Plainwell in 1865, was one of the stages of the Good Intent Line. The line probably was run by one of Mary Lewis's relatives. This advertisement was posted in towns throughout southern Michigan. Stagecoaches carried people from the railroad lines to small towns throughout the state.

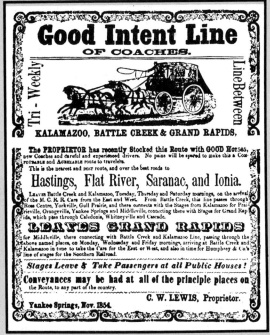

When Michigan became a state, Detroit looked like this. With 9,000 people, it was Michigan's largest city.

EARLY TOWNS

As more settlers arrived, towns began. Michigan's early villages sprang up for different reasons. Some grew along roads like the Chicago Road. Others grew beside a river where someone had built a water-powered mill. (The mill would grind flour or cut lumber for the settlers nearby.) Some villages grew around taverns. Others grew around early forts or the government land offices.

When Michigan became a state in 1837, Detroit, with 9,000 people, was its only incorporated, or formally organized city. There were 15 incorporated villages. In southeastern Michigan were Ann Arbor, Pontiac, Monroe, Mt. Clemens, Ypsilanti, Adrian and Tecumseh. In southcentral Michigan were Marshall and Coldwater. In southwestern Michigan were Niles, St. Joseph, White Pigeon, Constantine, Centreville and New Buffalo. Other growing settlements that had not been incorporated included Grand Rapids and Kalamazoo.

In those young communities, churches and newspapers were very important. They gave people a sense of belonging to their community. And they often brought news from other communities.

CHURCHES

When Michigan was a territory with mostly French settlers, most people belonged to the Roman Catholic Church. The

Father Gabriel Richard was a leader in religion and education. He also published Michigan's first newspaper. This is how Detroit's St. Anne's Roman Catholic Church once looked.

New England and New York settlers who came in the 1830s were mostly Protestants. They belonged to Methodist, Baptist, Presbyterian, Congregational, Episcopalian, Lutheran, Reformed and Quaker churches.

In small communities, people usually started a church by holding religious meetings in someone's home. Later they would find a pastor. In some churches, this pastor was a "circuit rider." The circuit rider served a number of communities. He rode his horse from place to place. He stayed at the home of one of the church members, preached a sermon, told what was happening in other villages and helped people with their problems. Then he rode on to the next community. Eventually,

when a group had enough members and money, it built a church.

NEWSPAPERS

In 1809, in Detroit, Father Gabriel Richard published Michigan's first newspaper, *The Michigan Essay or Impartial Observer.* It was hard to find support for a newspaper, and historians think Richard published only one issue of his paper. The first continuously published paper was the *Detroit Gazette.* It first appeared in 1817. The first newspaper started outside of Detroit was the *Monroe Sentinel.* It began in 1825.

Some men began what is now the state's oldest paper in 1831 in a small log cabin in

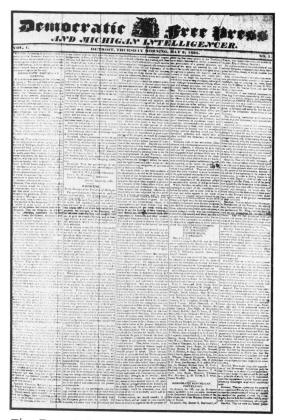

The Detroit Free Press *is Michigan's oldest existing newspaper. This is a picture of its first edition.*

Detroit. At first it was called the *Democratic Free Press and Michigan Intelligencer.* Today it is known as the *Detroit Free Press.* The oldest daily newspaper outside of Detroit is the *Kalamazoo Gazette.* When it began in 1835, it was called the *Michigan Statesman.*

An early newspaper usually had only two or four pages. It was printed once every week. One person often owned the paper, wrote for it and printed it. The typical printer copied stories from other papers from all over the nation. He often did not try to be fair or present both sides of a story. Instead he wrote articles that clearly favored his political party.

CONCLUSION

A flood of pioneers came to Michigan between 1830 and 1850. They came because the Erie Canal made traveling easier and because the government was selling good Michigan farmland for a low price. Many came from New York and New England. Others came from foreign countries like Holland, Ireland and Germany. Some came alone; others, such as the Beaver Island Mormons, the Dutch and the Cass County blacks, settled in groups.

Pioneer life was difficult. The land was hard to plow. Weather could destroy crops. But pioneers also had fun.

At first most farm products were used by the family. Later farmers began to sell some food to people in other parts of the country.

The pioneers built villages around taverns, saw and flour mills, land offices and forts. Churches and newspapers were important in those communities.

In the next chapter, Michigan's pioneers become involved in national problems—slavery and the Civil War.

THE STOMACH WITH A WINDOW

Mackinac Island was not a likely place for medical discoveries in the 1820s and 1830s. It was still a wilderness area. But a pioneering doctor did important medical research there.

The story began on June 6, 1822, in the retail store of the island's most important business—William Astor's fur trading company. At the Astor store Alexis St. Martin was accidentally wounded by a shotgun blast.

Fort Mackinac's surgeon, Dr. William Beaumont, was called. At first Beaumont thought he could not save St. Martin. But St. Martin lived.

There was one problem, however. The shotgun blast had opened a three-inch hole in St. Martin's stomach. After St. Martin had recovered from all his other wounds, the hole was still there. Dr. Beaumont kept a bandage over the hole.

He could remove the bandage and see St. Martin's stomach at work and remove partly digested food.

Dr. Beaumont wrote about how St. Martin's digestive system worked. He conducted experiments. His reports were read by other doctors.

St. Martin continued an active life. He married, was the father of many children and was still alive when Dr. Beaumont died in 1853. St. Martin died in 1880.

THE NEXT STORY

When this chapter starts, the northern states and southern states are arguing with each other about extending slavery to new states. They cannot agree, and the Civil War breaks out. The war affects many Michigan men and women.

PEOPLE

Sam Hodgman was a young man from Climax, Michigan, who volunteered to be a soldier.

Adam Crosswhite was an escaped slave who settled near Marshall with his family. Some southerners came north and tried to capture him.

Abraham Lincoln was president of the United States during the war.

Austin Blair was governor of Michigan when the Civil War started.

PLACES

Climax, a village in southern Michigan, was Sam Hodgman's hometown.

Jackson was the place where the Republican party was organized in 1854.

The Sault Locks made it possible for ships to go from Lake Superior to Lake Huron.

WORDS

Under **slavery** white people owned black people called **slaves.** Owners could buy and sell slaves and make them do any kind of work.

The **Underground Railway** was not a railroad. It was an informal organization that helped slaves escape from their owners.

To **secede** is to leave or quit being part of a group. Just before the Civil War, some southern states seceded from the United States.

The **Confederacy** was the name given the southern states that seceded. They were also called the South.

The **Union** was the name for the states that remained part of the United States during the Civil War. They were also called the North.

The **cavalry** is an army unit in which the soldiers ride horses while fighting.

The **infantry** is an army unit in which the soldiers go into battle on foot.

WHEN DID IT HAPPEN?

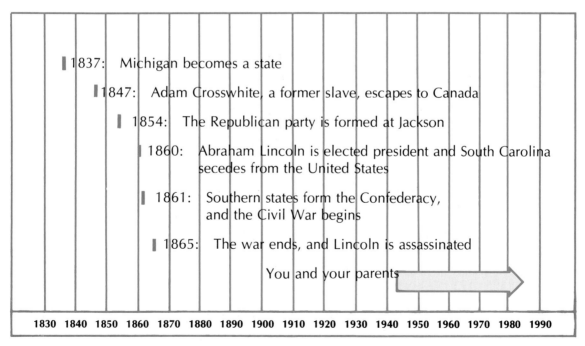

1837: Michigan becomes a state

1847: Adam Crosswhite, a former slave, escapes to Canada

1854: The Republican party is formed at Jackson

1860: Abraham Lincoln is elected president and South Carolina secedes from the United States

1861: Southern states form the Confederacy, and the Civil War begins

1865: The war ends, and Lincoln is assassinated

You and your parents

1830 1840 1850 1860 1870 1880 1890 1900 1910 1920 1930 1940 1950 1960 1970 1980 1990

CHAPTER EIGHT MICHIGAN AND THE CIVIL WAR

It was September 17, 1862. Sam Hodgman had been in the Union army for over a year, but he had not been in any battles. Now his regiment, the Seventh Michigan Infantry, was moving into position near Sharpsburg, Maryland. The soldiers encountered little resistance as they moved toward a wooded area.

Suddenly rebel guns opened up. As the men began falling, Sam tried to rally his comrades. Later he wrote to his parents, "The [musket balls] were flying all around . . . and like plums in a pudding were bursting in every direction. It seemed almost a miracle that anyone escaped."

Sam was wounded in both legs. Eventually, he hobbled to a field hospital two miles behind the lines. A week later he was moved to an army hospital in Philadelphia.

Sam had lived through the bloodiest single day of the Civil War—the Battle of Antietam. Some 25,000 soldiers from the North and the South were killed, wounded or captured that day. Of Sam's unit of 360, only 138 were unhurt.

Susan Price

BEFORE THE WAR

Sam, like most young men from Michigan, had grown up hearing people talk about slavery. The southern states allowed people to own black slaves, but most northern states did not. The South wanted slavery to be allowed in some of the territories and new states of the United States. They feared that if this did not happen, they would soon be outnumbered in the U.S. Congress. Then the Congress might adopt laws that would harm the slave system.

Some people in Michigan opposed this expansion of slavery. Others wanted to completely end slavery. Some fought against slavery by helping fugitive slaves escape from the South.

THE UNDERGROUND RAILWAY

The Underground Railway was the name given to the informal system of roads and homes used to help slaves escape from their southern masters. Most towns in southern Michigan had people who took part. They hid escaping slaves in their homes and barns during the day. Then, at night, they moved them to houses or barns in the next town. Some of the slaves went to Canada. Some chose to stay in Michigan.

Sometimes southern slave owners tried to capture their escaped slaves. One example of this involved Adam Crosswhite, an escaped slave who settled near Marshall in Calhoun County.

Crosswhite was a fugitive from Kentucky. He feared that someone from Kentucky might try to take him and his family back to slavery. So he arranged a danger signal with his neighbors.

This poster sought farm tools to help escaped slaves begin new lives.

One morning in 1847 the neighbors heard the signal. They ran to his house. At the door were four Kentucky men and a law officer from the Marshall area.

The neighbors managed to help the Crosswhites and their four children escape by train to Detroit and then to Canada.

The Kentuckians were angry. In court they charged the Marshall leaders with keeping them from regaining their legal property. The Marshall leaders had to pay fines to the slave owners. In 1850, the United States passed a fugitive slave law to make it clearly illegal for people like the Marshall leaders to help escaping slaves. Michigan did not like the law. In 1855, Michigan passed a law that said state and local officials could not help people trying to capture fugitive slaves.

Many Michigan people opposed slavery. But that did not mean that they thought blacks and whites were equal. In 1850 the state's white men refused to give black men the right to vote. At that time no women were allowed to vote either.

This home in Union City was one of the stops on the Underground Railway. Slaves escaping from the South would be hidden there until they could be moved on. Among the former slaves who moved to Michigan was Sojourner Truth (right). Making her home in Battle Creek, she spoke against slavery throughout the North. After the Civil War, she spoke for rights for blacks and women.

THE REPUBLICAN PARTY

In the summer of 1854, Michigan people who opposed extending slavery decided to meet at Jackson. They had been members of the Democratic, Whig and Free Soil political parties.

About 1,500 people came to the meeting. That was far more than expected. No meeting hall in Jackson was big enough to hold them. So they met under the trees near the corner of Franklin and Second streets in downtown Jackson. There they formed the Republican party. Soon people in other states joined the party.

In the 1860 presidential election, Republican Abraham Lincoln defeated three other candidates. In Michigan, Lincoln received 88,450 votes; Democrat Stephen Douglas was second with 64,958.

During the campaign, Lincoln opposed extending slavery to territories and new states. The southern states saw this as an attack on their way of life. And seven weeks after Lincoln won the election, South Carolina seceded from the Union. It declared that it was no longer part of the United States. Eventually eleven other states joined South Carolina. They formed the Confederate States of America.

THE CIVIL WAR BEGINS

The Civil War began on April 12, 1861, when Southern forces fired on and captured Fort Sumter, a United States post. The fort was on an island in Charleston Harbor, South Carolina.

Sam Hodgman, like many Michigan men, was excited when the war began. He organized a company of volunteer soldiers

Samuel Hodgman of Climax was among the first Michigan men to sign up to fight for the North in the Civil War. He served in the 7th Michigan Infantry until March 1864.

in his hometown, Climax. Although they were not yet in the army, Sam drilled his men regularly in the village. He could not wait to join the army and fight.

Right after the attack on Fort Sumter, President Lincoln asked each state to send volunteer troops to the capital of the United States, Washington, D.C.

Michigan had to find men. It also had to find weapons, clothes and equipment for them. The state had no money in the treasury, and the legislature was not in session. Governor Austin Blair started a campaign to raise $100,000 from private groups and

When the war first started, many people thought it would end quickly. Michigan was swept up in a surge of patriotic fever. Here hundreds turn out to watch Michigan's First Volunteer Infantry Regiment accept flags that it would carry into battle. But it was not a short nor an easy war. Many men died on both sides.

people. Later the legislature repaid these people. The state raised $81,020 this way.

Only 16 days after Fort Sumter fell, the state had enough men at Fort Wayne in Detroit to form the First Michigan Volunteers. After two weeks of training, the men were sent to Washington, D.C. A story is told that when Lincoln saw these troops, he said, "Thank God for Michigan."

Three more Michigan regiments were quickly trained and sent to Washington. By June 1861, the U.S. had about 80,000 soldiers in the Washington area, but most were poorly trained. They saw their first action on July 21. That day the Union lost the Battle of Bull Run, in northern Virginia.

Michigan people supported the Union in the war for many reasons.

1. Many Republicans and people who had worked in the Underground Railway wanted the war to end slavery.
2. Other people believed you could not let parts of your country decide to form a new country. They supported the war to preserve the Union.
3. With few southern friends or business dealings, most Michigan people had little sympathy for the South.

SAM HODGMAN ENLISTS

The first Michigan soldiers had already been in Washington for a month when the army told Sam Hodgman that he and his men could enlist. On June 22, Sam became first sergeant of Company I, Seventh Michigan Infantry, at Fort Wayne in Detroit.

Sam liked camp life. The soldiers rose at 4:30 A.M., ate breakfast, drilled all morning, ate lunch, rested until 3 P.M., drilled some more, ate dinner, paraded at 7 P.M. and went to bed at 9 P.M.

"It's like a picnic," one of Sam's buddies said. "It's so romantic for us all who have been accustomed to hard work on the farm."

In August the Seventh Infantry with its 884 men took a train to Washington. In October, they were sent to Virginia.

THE WAR IS NO LONGER A PICNIC

The Civil War was fought in two parts of the country. In the east, where Sam Hodgman was, the Northern forces unsuccessfully tried to capture the Confederate capital, Richmond. Next, Confederate troops under Robert E. Lee invaded western Maryland. In the west, the Union attacked border states and then tried to split the Old South from states like Texas by controlling the Mississippi River. Michigan troops fought in both parts of the country.

The first great battle in the west took place at Shiloh in southwestern Tennessee. There the Twelfth Michigan was part of the division that held on just long enough for Union reinforcements to arrive and save the northern army from defeat.

Warfare is often boring. While awaiting a battle, the soldiers had little to do. Here they pose for a picture.

Sam Hodgman was wounded in the Union's first important victory in the east, Antietam. The Union victory stopped Lee's first attempt to invade the North. It also gave President Lincoln the occasion to issue the Emancipation Proclamation.

This proclamation abolished slavery in the Confederate states, but not in those areas that had not seceded. It did not help many slaves at the time. But it meant that ending slavery had become an official goal of the North. All slaves would not be guaranteed freedom until the thirteenth amendment to the U.S. Constitution was ratified in 1865.

Michiganians fought in all the war's major battles. The 21st Michigan (above) fought at Perryville, Murfreesboro and Chickamauga. The men in this unit came from Upper Peninsula and northwestern Lower Peninsula counties. At least one woman was among Michigan's soldiers. Sarah Emma Edmonds (right) of Flint disguised herself as a man and enlisted. For some time she played her role as a man and took part in several battles. She also was said to have acted as a northern spy. She was in the army for two years.

FINDING MORE SOLDIERS

Despite some Union victories, the war dragged on. It became hard to find new men to join the army. People were discouraged because of the length of the war and because so many men had died.

First the federal government offered a bonus of extra money to people who joined the army. This did not get enough men, and in 1863 Congress passed a "draft" law. The new law said that each geographical area had to send a certain number of men to the army. If not enough men volunteered, some men from that area would be drafted (forced to join the army). The system was not very fair. Drafted men could pay $300 or find a substitute and not join the army.

In August 1863, President Lincoln also decided to allow blacks to join the army. Until then, many blacks had been cooks or medical attendants, but they had not been allowed to fight. In Detroit, 895 blacks immediately volunteered for the army. By March 1864, the First Michigan Colored Infantry had 1,600 men. Members of the First fought in several battles in the South that year.

THE TURNING POINTS OF 1863

In July 1863 the Union won important victories in the west and the east. In the west, General Ulysses S. Grant took Vicksburg, Mississippi, after a long siege. The Union now controlled the Mississippi River, which split the South in two.

In the east, Lee was again leading his southern troops around Washington, D.C. He met the Union troops at Gettysburg, Pennsylvania. Sam Hodgman was among

When President Lincoln decided blacks could serve in the Army, one of those who volunteered was Kinchen Artis of Detroit.

those troops. He had rejoined the Seventh Michigan Infantry in January. In June he had been promoted to captain.

The Battle of Gettysburg lasted three days, and many Michigan men fought in it. On the first day, eighty percent of the men in the Twenty-fourth Michigan Infantry were killed or wounded.

In another part of the battle, 24-year-old George A. Custer of Monroe led the Michigan Cavalry Brigade in a daring charge that helped save the Union Army from defeat.

On the third day, Sam's unit, the Seventh Michigan Infantry, was on Cemetery Ridge in the middle of the Union line. About

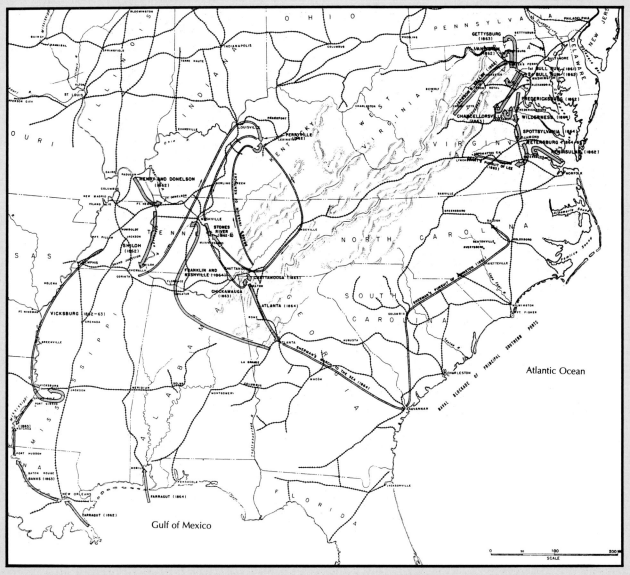

Michigan men and some women fought at all the Civil War's major battles.

10 A.M. the fighting stopped. Sam wondered if the battle had ended. It had not.

Around noon the Confederates began firing cannon at Cemetery Ridge. They fired for two hours. Then, about 15,000 Confederates moved out of the trees less than a mile away and charged across open fields to the Union line. Only a few Confederates made it to the clump of trees to the right of Sam and the Seventh. There the fighting was hand to hand, with bayonets.

When the battle ended, the Union forces had won. Sam counted his men. One third of them were dead or wounded.

Sam had grown tired of army life. Later that year he wrote home, "I am pretty well worn in the service. All tell me I look ten years older than I did when I joined the regiment."

In March 1864, Sam was honorably discharged. He had not fully recovered from the typhoid fever he caught while in the army. His leg wounds also bothered him. Of the 884 men of the Seventh who had so cheerfully left Michigan in 1861 when Sam joined the army, only 160 were left.

Sam was an average Civil War soldier. Like so many others, he had learned that war, which often seemed exciting, was in reality tragic.

THE WAR'S END

In the west, two great battles were fought in Tennessee and Georgia in 1863. Michigan men played important roles in both. Many died in the Union's September defeat at Chickamauga. Others helped build a pontoon bridge so northern troops trapped in Chattanooga could get food and

Colonel Benjamin Pritchard of Allegan led the 4th Michigan Cavalry, which captured Confederate President Jefferson Davis.

supplies. Still others were with the Eleventh Michigan Infantry as it stormed up Missionary Ridge in the Union's victory at the Battle of Chattanooga in November.

Now the west was secure. Lee had been forced back to the South after Gettysburg. The Union began its final attack.

In the east, Union troops commanded by Grant began slowly to push south. In the west, under William T. Sherman, the Union troops marched through Georgia then north to meet Grant.

Finally, on April 9, 1865, General Lee surrendered to General Grant at Appomattox Court House in central Virginia. The war was over.

The president of the defeated Confederacy, Jefferson Davis, fled south. Colonel

Michigan women helped the soldiers by operating this sanitary station in northern Virginia. Austin Blair (right), who was governor of Michigan throughout most of the Civil War, used his own money to buy supplies for Michigan soldiers.

Benjamin Pritchard of Allegan and the Fourth Michigan Cavalry captured him near Irwinville, Georgia, on May 10, 1865.

THE WAR IN MICHIGAN

During the Civil War, people at home helped the soldiers. They sent packages of food, bandages and medical supplies to men and hospitals. They helped the needy families of men away at war. Many doctors offered free medical service to families of army men.

Governor Blair spent his own money on supplies for Michigan soldiers. In 1865 he left the governorship a poorer man than when he entered it.

Michigan farmers were beginning to use new labor-saving machines. With the help of the machinery and good weather, they raised a lot of wheat, corn, oats and rye to feed the soldiers and their horses.

Copper and iron were needed to make cannon, guns and ammunition for the soldiers. Fortunately for the Union, the canal and locks at Sault Ste. Marie had been opened in 1855. This meant that ships could easily carry iron and copper from Michigan's Upper Peninsula through the Great Lakes to cities where weapons were manufactured. Michigan copper was so important that its price almost tripled during the war.

During the war years, the volume of goods produced by Michigan factories almost doubled. The war forced prices up, but wages stayed low.

The celebration in the North to mark the war's end was abruptly halted when President Abraham Lincoln was shot on 14 April 1865. Memorial services were held for the slain leader all across Michigan. Above Detroiters gather to pay their last respects.

AFTER THE WAR

As the North began to celebrate the end of the war, it was suddenly plunged into sadness. On April 14, just five days after Lee's surrender, President Lincoln was killed by John Wilkes Booth. Memorial services were held in cities and villages throughout Michigan.

After Lincoln's death Michigan and the nation began to rebuild. Some 90,000 Michigan men had served in the army and navy during the Civil War. Nearly 14,000 died, some by gunfire, but many by disease and illness. Every town had both widows and war heroes.

CONCLUSION

Before the Civil War, people in Michigan had strong opinions about slavery. Some helped slaves escape along the Underground Railway. Many met at Jackson to form the Republican party, which opposed the extension of slavery.

When the war began, Michigan was solidly behind the Union war effort. Many Michigan people joined the army to preserve the Union. Some also hoped the war would end slavery. It did both.

Young men like Sam Hodgman thought the war would be an exciting adventure. They found out that it was a sad experience, filled with boredom, illness, suffering and death.

Michigan's farms, mines and businesses contributed greatly to the war effort. In the next two chapters we will see what happened to two Michigan industries—lumbering and mining—after the war.

George Armstrong Custer of Monroe was only twenty-four years old when he became a brigadier general. He commanded the Michigan Cavalry Brigade in 1863 and 1864. After the war, he left and then rejoined the army. He is best remembered as the man who led 264 cavalry men to their deaths at the Battle of the Little Big Horn in Montana in 1876.

THE NEXT STORY

In this chapter Michigan develops its lumbering industry. Lumber brings the state great riches. But the lumber companies and fires destroy many beautiful forests. It takes many years for Michigan to replant and manage its forests.

PEOPLE

George Erickson was a Michigan lumberjack.

Scott Gerrish introduced Michigan's first successful narrow-gauge railroad to the lumber industry.

Silas Overpack of Manistee invented a big cart to carry huge piles of logs.

PLACES

Clare is one of many towns that grew because of the lumber boom.

Hartwick Pines State Park, near **Grayling**, has a replica of a lumber camp amid a virgin pine forest.

Holland was the site of Michigan's first great forest fire in 1871. Other towns that suffered from fires were **Manistee, Metz, Au Sable** and **Oscoda**.

Grand Rapids and **Port Huron** were on the northern edge of settlement until the lumber boom began.

Escanaba, Menominee, Muskegon, Traverse City, Saginaw and **Bay City** were some of the Michigan towns where logs were sawed into boards.

WORDS

The **Super Pine Belt** was the area in the north central part of the Lower Peninsula in which the best pine trees were found.

Drivers or **river hogs** guided the logs as they floated down the river.

Lumberjacks or **shanty boys** were the men who cut down the trees.

A **timber cruiser** was a man who went into the forests to find good stands of trees to cut down.

A **virgin forest** is one that has not been cut by man.

Cutover land was what was left after loggers cut down a forest.

WHEN DID IT HAPPEN?

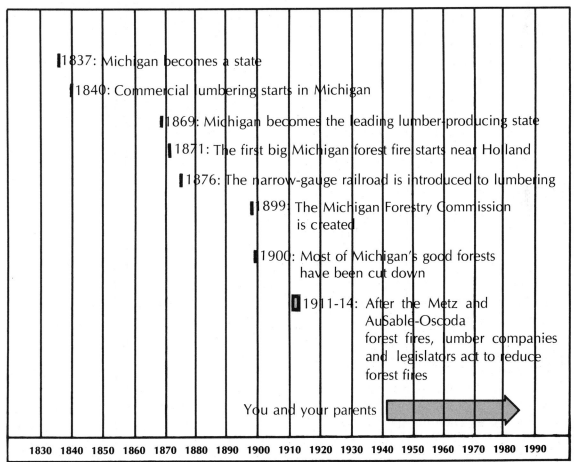

1837: Michigan becomes a state

1840: Commercial lumbering starts in Michigan

1869: Michigan becomes the leading lumber-producing state

1871: The first big Michigan forest fire starts near Holland

1876: The narrow-gauge railroad is introduced to lumbering

1899: The Michigan Forestry Commission is created

1900: Most of Michigan's good forests have been cut down

1911-14: After the Metz and AuSable-Oscoda forest fires, lumber companies and legislators act to reduce forest fires

You and your parents

1830	1840	1850	1860	1870	1880	1890	1900	1910	1920	1930	1940	1950	1960	1970	1980	1990

CHAPTER NINE
TIMBER!

Standing at the foot of the giant pine tree, George Erickson wore a dark, short jacket, heavy gray wool pants and high leather boots. He had a red sash tied around his waist.

George was a lumberjack. He and the other lumberjacks were also called shanty boys. They earned that nickname because they ate their meals and spent their nights in shanties.

George and another shanty boy were standing in the snow at the foot of a giant white pine tree in Clare County. If you had put a tape measure around the tree, it would have measured almost four feet. The tree was 120 feet tall.

With his axe, George cut a wide V-shaped notch in the tree trunk. He cut the notch on the side toward which he wanted the tree to fall.

Then George and his friend moved to the tree's other side. Against the trunk, they placed the teeth of their seven-foot-long saw. George stood at one end of the saw. His companion stood at the other. Back and forth they moved the saw.

As the saw neared the notch, they heard the tree trunk cracking. "Timber-r-r-r!" George shouted. That single word told everyone, "Get out of the way!"

In 1875, George and his companion were among many men cutting down thousands of Michigan trees. George was 22 and unmarried. He wanted to start a blacksmith shop some day. He had come from a farm near Detroit. In Clare County he hoped to earn enough money to start his shop. He earned $28 a month, plus food and a bed. That was fairly good pay in those days, but to earn it, George had to work from dawn to dusk.

LUMBERING BEGINS

When white people first came to Michigan, most of the land was covered with trees. Some said a squirrel could travel on tree branches for hundreds of miles without ever touching the ground.

The early settlers did not see trees as a way to make money. They cut them down to build homes and barns and fences. They cut them or burned them down to clear fields so they could grow crops. They also burned wood for heat and cooking. But they did not cut trees for lumber to sell to other people.

Around 1840 Michigan men began to cut trees to sell. They sawed the trees into boards and sold them to people in towns. This was called commercial lumbering.

Before 1840 most commercial lumbering was done in New York and Maine. But as the eastern trees were cut and as people moved west, new sources of lumber were needed. Michigan was ready.

By 1869—right after the Civil War—Michigan had become the nation's leading producer of lumber. For thirty years it continued to lead the nation. In those years Michigan trees produced more dollars than did California's gold.

THE SUPER PINE BELT

The lumber industry brought settlers to northern Michigan. Until lumbering began, virtually all of Michigan's people lived in the southern part of the state. Hardly anyone lived north of an imaginary line that ran from Grand Rapids to Port Huron.

One of the busiest of those new towns in the north was Clare. At one point in the late

HARDWOODS

MIXED HARDWOODS & CONIFERS

PINE PLAINS, JACK, NORWAY AND WHITE PINE

PINE FLATS, HEMLOCK, SPRUCE FIR, CEDAR AND WHITE PINE

WET AND DRY RUGGED LAND, FOREST MIXED

SWAMP

Between 1870 and 1900, Michigan led the nation in lumber production. Since it floated, pine was cut first. Later devices, like narrow-gauge railroads, allowed hardwoods to be cut.

1870s, one hundred and fifty logging camps were operating within ten miles of Clare. George Erickson worked in one of these camps.

In 1871, Clare County had a population of fewer than 500. Twenty years later, its population was 7,558. The people came to Clare because it was part of the "super pine belt" that ran across the central Lower Peninsula. The pine belt's lumber was more

Lumbermen sometimes competed to see which lumber camp could produce the biggest load of logs. The logs were carefully stacked on sleds and bound together with chains. The horses would pull the sleds on a road made of ice to a nearby river. Driving the sled was dangerous and required great skill. After the ice and snow melted in the spring, the logs would be floated downstream to a sawmill where they would be cut.

in demand than any other wood. Pine was soft. Carpenters liked working with it. Also, pine logs could float down rivers to saw-mills and Great Lakes ports. Logs of hardwoods, like oak and maple, would sink and it was expensive to carry them over roads and railroads.

The forests of good white pine were found by men called "timber cruisers." The timber cruisers tramped through the forest for weeks at a time. They climbed tall trees to see better. When they found good stands of pines, they marked them on government land maps and hurried back to a government land office. There they bought the land for their bosses.

A smart timber cruiser could help the owner of a lumber company become a mil-lionaire. A few timber cruisers became lumbermen and millionaires themselves.

This crew of shanty boys posed in front of the shanties in which they lived. The buildings had practically no windows and each was heated by a single stove. A camp might have several bunkhouses, a cook shanty, a blacksmith shop and a company store.

THE SHANTY BOYS

George Erickson worked in a typical lumber camp. It had a bunkhouse, as well as a shanty in which the men ate. It also had stables for the oxen and horses and a blacksmith shop. The camp store and the office for the camp foreman were in the same building.

The bunkhouse had two rows of bunks along the walls. A wood stove stood in the center. George slept in an upper bunk about four feet off the floor. He did not have the kind of mattress we use today. The slats of his bunk were made of small boards. Over these slats, George' put cedar and hemlock boughs. On top of that was a straw-filled tick (a type of mattress).

In cold weather, smoke from the stove filtered through the bunkhouse. But it was easy to sleep because everyone was tired.

Each night, George and the others traded stories and played cards in the bunkhouse. But the fun could not last long. Everyone had to be in bed by nine o'clock so he could get up in the morning at five o'clock.

The bunkhouse stories included many about Paul Bunyan. The shanty boys made up fantastic stories about Paul and his imaginary blue ox, Babe. Each time the shanty boys told a story, Paul Bunyan and Babe got taller and stronger.

The shanty boys were mostly single men between twenty and thirty years old. Many of Michigan's first shanty boys came from

Many logging camps had company stores (left). In the springtime, river hogs (right) floated logs that had been cut the previous winter to sawmills. Because they often walked on the slippery logs, river hogs had dangerous jobs.

the pine belts of New England, New York, Pennsylvania and Canada. But soon they were joined by sons of Michigan farmers, Indians and immigrants.

THE RIVER HOGS

While George Erickson and his companions cut down trees, other men hauled the logs off on horse-drawn sleighs. Each log was cut to the same length—sixteen feet. They were then hauled to the bank of a nearby river. There the men marked the end of each log with the lumber company's brand. This way each company knew which logs it owned.

In the spring, when the ice on the river melted, the logs were floated down the river to a sawmill. As they floated, they were watched by "drivers" or "river hogs." The drivers' job was to keep the logs moving.

Sometimes the logs would get caught on a sand bank or an overhanging branch. Hundreds of logs would jam up and stop moving. The drivers would have to free the logs that were causing the jam. Walking on the slippery, moving logs was fast, dangerous work.

A floating cookhouse followed the logs on the larger rivers. It looked like a houseboat and was called a wanigan by the drivers. Sometimes the men took turns sleeping there. Each driver usually ate breakfast and supper at the cookhouse.

Before the logs reached the sawmill, each one was marked with a special company brand. The logs for each company were sorted out in the river and guided to a special pen. From that pen, each company's logs could be floated as a group to the sawmill. This Muskegon sawmill was built in 1873.

SORT-AND-BOOM

When the logs neared the mouth of the logging rivers, they were sorted out. The brand on the end of each log was checked to see who owned the log. The logs belonging to each owner were floated to that owner's "pen." A pen was formed in the water by chaining together some huge floating logs. These pens were called booms.

After a certain number of logs were gathered within a boom, they were fastened together into a long raft. This raft would be floated on down the river to the sawmill.

SAWMILLS

Sawmills were usually located along major rivers or where a river entered a lake. There were large mills at Escanaba, Menominee, Muskegon, Traverse City, Saginaw and Bay City, to name a few. At the mill, the logs were cut into boards. From the mills, the lumber was sent all over the country by ship or railroad.

At first logging was done only in the winter when loads of logs were moved by sled. It became a year-round operation when Silas Overpack of Manistee invented the "big wheel." Big wheels allowed logs to be moved when there was no ice or snow. Logging brands like these at left made it possible to sort the logs that floated downstream each spring.

Saginaw River mills cut the logs from George Erickson's camp. In 1880 there were 32 of these mills near Bay City. And in 1888 Saginaw River mills cut over four billion board feet of lumber—enough to build a four-foot sidewalk around the world four times.

LOGGING CHANGES

Several inventions helped Michigan's lumber industry grow. Until the 1870s most trees were cut down with axes. About 1870 two-man crosscut saws were improved so they could be used to cut standing timber. This speeded up the work.

Silas Overpack of Manistee contributed a cart called a "big wheel." The cart had wheels that were ten feet across, almost twice as tall as a man. The wheels had steel rims six inches wide. The tongue, or bottom part of the cart, was sixteen feet long. Logs could be slung in over the tongue, chained together and hauled away when there was no snow or ice.

133

The first Michigan narrow-gauge logging railroad was built in 1876. Eventually Michigan had 89 narrow-gauge railroads. The railroads made it possible to move logs to sawmills year-round. They also allowed loggers to move hardwoods that did not float like pine.

LOGGING RAILROADS

Commercial lumbering in the early days was a wintertime activity. Logs were hauled by sleigh over the snow and ice to a nearby river. The logs were too heavy to drag over dirt. Most of the lumbering camps were located close to rivers.

But in 1876 geared locomotives and narrow-gauge railroads changed lumbering. The engines and cars on narrow-gauge railroads were smaller, lighter and cheaper than those on standard-gauge railroads. The engines could run on tight curves and uneven tracks. The rails for the tracks were lighter and closer together. They could be pulled up and moved once the trees around

them were gone. The new portable railroads allowed lumbermen to work all year long. They also meant that lumbermen could work farther away from rivers.

One of the first narrow-gauge logging railroads in the nation was built by Scott Gerrish. He built it in the area between Clare and Lake George. It became very successful and other such railroads soon followed. By 1889, there were 89 such railroads in Michigan.

LOGGING PROBLEMS

The lumber industry brought millions of dollars to Michigan, but it also brought many problems.

134

The lumber industry used up entire Michigan forests. The land it left behind was called "cutover" because all that was left were stumps like these. Many years would pass before Michigan began to replant and manage its forest resources.

Lumberjacks worked long, hard hours. Sometimes their food was not good. Their beds were not comfortable. Some protested by quitting work. They called it going on strike. But there were always other men looking for jobs, so lumber camp owners simply hired new men to do the work. Working conditions did not change much.

Lumberjacks were well known for celebrating too much when they finally left the isolated lumber camps and came in to towns like Clare. In logging areas, there were few sheriffs and many chances to break the law. Many men drank too much alcohol. Some were involved in fights, murders and robberies. Others cut logs from other people's land. Still others stole logs, cut off the brands and put their own brands on them.

THE DECLINE OF LUMBERING

Another problem caused by lumbering was that entire forests were destroyed. Michigan and states west of it had so many trees that no one worried about planting more trees.

The logging railroads speeded up the destruction of Michigan's forests. Before railroads, only pine trees near rivers were cut. After railroads, all the trees could be cut. And hardwood trees, like oak and maple, could be shipped without using the rivers.

When the lumbermen cut down the forests, they left behind piles of dried brush and sawdust. The fires that started in these areas could destroy whole towns or counties. In 1908, one of Michigan's worst fires left Metz looking like this.

Some people worried about lumber for the future. In 1899 the Michigan legislature created the Michigan Forestry Commission. The commission was supposed to check on the lumber industry. But it was too late to stop the destruction of the forests. It would be many years before people began to re-plant the forests.

As the twentieth century began, most of the best Michigan forests were gone. Michigan no longer led the nation in lumbering. Many of the lumber owners and shanty boys had moved west to the forests of Wisconsin, Minnesota, Oregon and Washington.

In Michigan, lumber towns died. Store fronts were boarded up. Some places became ghost towns.

The cutover land the lumberjacks left behind was marked by stumps and piles of dry, broken branches. These, too, would cause problems.

FIRES

The loggers had not worried about cleaning up the stumps and tree branches they could not use. As these dried out, they became a fire hazard.

The first great Michigan fire occurred in 1871. It had been an extremely hot and dry

136

At Metz, fire that warped the railroad tracks caused a rescue train to crash. Fifteen people died on the train.

summer. Some fires were started by a spark from machinery or a railroad train. Some started because someone was burning brush to clear land for farming. Others started because the sun made dry wood so hot, it began to burn. On October 8 fire broke out near Holland. During the night the wind grew strong, and the fire raced into town. The fire destroyed most of the town. Only one person died, but three hundred families lost their homes.

Farther north along the lake, a fire in Manistee destroyed half the town. From there, the fires were fanned by strong winds. They raced east across the state.

Fields, homes and forests were scorched in Lake, Osceola, Isabella, Midland, Saginaw, Tuscola, Sanilac and Huron counties. The homes of 18,000 persons were destroyed.

Ten years later, in 1881, the Thumb area burned. The fires took 282 lives and destroyed a million acres.

In the next 27 years, fires occurred almost every year. But they did not destroy much property nor cause many deaths. As a result, not much was done to control or prevent fires.

That all changed because of what happened at Metz on a hot, dry October day in 1908. Metz is located in the northeastern part of the Lower Peninsula.

The fire began west of Metz. On October 15, it reached the edge of town. In three hours the town had burned to the ground. The fire then spread north, south and east.

Before the fire burned out, forty-two people had died. Fifteen of them died when the rescue train in which they were trying to escape ran off the rails. The wreck was caused because the railroad tracks had been warped by the heat of the fire.

Two years later, Michigan's last large fire destroyed the Lake Huron towns of Au Sable and Oscoda. Twenty people died in that fire.

The Metz and Au Sable-Oscoda fires convinced people that something needed to be done to prevent fires. In 1911, lumbermen began hiring fire wardens to look for fires on their property.

In 1912, the state legislature began forest fire programs. These programs included preventing and fighting fires as well as watching out for them.

The men who owned lumber companies usually made a lot of money. They often built big, expensive homes with fancy details. The home above was built in Muskegon by lumberman Charles H. Hackley. Many of the forests that lumber companies destroyed have been replanted. The photograph at left shows workers in the 1950s weeding seed beds of pine trees. The seedlings were later planted in the cutover lands.

REBUILDING THE FORESTS

It took centuries for Michigan's forests to grow. But it took only fifty years for the lumber companies to destroy most of them.

By 1900 there were only a few virgin forests—forests that were not cut and replanted by men.

The Upper Peninsula still has a few virgin forests, both state-owned and privately owned. The best-known virgin forest, however, is located in the Lower Peninsula. It is the 85-acre Hartwick Pines State Park north of Grayling. The state has built a replica of a lumber camp there.

During the peak of the lumbering era, when the companies finished cutting down the trees in a region, they abandoned the region. Later they tried to sell this cutover land to the settlers. But much of the cutover land was not good for farming. The settlers, too, had to abandon it.

Whenever settlers and lumber companies did not pay their taxes, the state took the land over. As a result, the amount of state-owned land in the northern part of Michigan grew. Today it is part of the state and national forest systems.

During this century, the state of Michigan began growing new forests. In 1903, the legislature created the office of forest warden. The warden was to supervise the regrowth of forests, as well as the existing forest preserves. The first two counties effected were Crawford and Roscommon.

Today Michigan has one of the largest state forest programs in the nation. Half the land area of Michigan is classified as forest.

About one-third of it is owned by the state and federal governments. On both private and public lands, scientifically controlled tree farms are becoming more important.

The lumber industry still exists in Michigan. Hardwood trees, such as maple, oak and birch, are used for fine furniture. Fast-growing trees, such as aspen, supply pulpwood for paper. Wood for use as charcoal fuel is sold in great amounts, too. And there are still many sawmills in the state.

CONCLUSION

The lumber industry brought people and millions of dollars to northern Michigan. Lumberjacks or shanty boys cut down white pine trees, then floated the logs down rivers to sawmills.

Two-man crosscut saws, big wheel carts and logging railroads helped loggers cut down more trees.

Lumbering also created problems. Lumber camps were not pleasant places to live and lumbering towns were often lawless places. When the forests were destroyed, the loggers moved on, leaving behind acres of stumps and brush and abandoned towns. When the brush caught fire, there were terrible forest fires.

After 1900, Michigan began to try to prevent fires. It also started to replant and preserve its forests. Today, forestry is an important Michigan industry and Michigan has a large state forest program.

In the next chapters we will see how Michigan developed another natural resource industry, mining.

Fort Wilkins
Calumet
Houghton
Lake Superior
Negaunee
Soo Canal
Fayette
Lake Huron
Rogers City
Midland
Saginaw
Grand Rapids
Lansing
Detroit

THE NEXT STORY

In this chapter, a three-ton copper boulder and iron ore that makes the needle of a compass spin around open Michigan's mining boom. While lumbermen cut down trees above the ground, miners find copper, iron, salt, gypsum, limestone and a little gold and silver beneath the ground. As Michigan mines these underground riches, it builds new towns, railroads and a canal.

PEOPLE

Alexander Henry was the first white man to see the Ontonagon Boulder.

Julius Eldred was the man who finally moved the Ontonagon Boulder.

Douglass Houghton was the geologist who decided copper could be mined in the Upper Peninsula.

William Austin Burt found iron ore while surveying in the Upper Peninsula.

Cornish immigrants (from Cornwall in England) brought mining skills and pasties to Michigan.

Herbert Henry Dow separated various chemicals from salt brine and founded the Dow Chemical Company in Midland.

PLACES

Houghton and **Fort Wilkins** were in the Copper Country.

William Burt found iron at **Negaunee**.

Fayette was an iron smelting town.

Iron was shipped from **Marquette**.

The **Soo Canal** allowed ships to easily move between **Lake Superior** and **Lake Huron**.

There were mines and quarries at **Rogers City**, **Grand Rapids**, **Midland** and **Saginaw**.

WORDS

A **mine shaft** is an opening that runs deep into the ground to the location of the ore or mineral being mined.

A **compass** has a needle that always points north. It is used to tell directions.

In a **strike**, workers refuse to work unless the employer grants their demands. The demands may be for better pay or working conditions.

Pig iron is made when iron ore is heated in a forge or furnace in order to separate the iron from the rest of the rock.

Locks are used to raise and lower ships between two bodies of water.

WHEN DID IT HAPPEN?

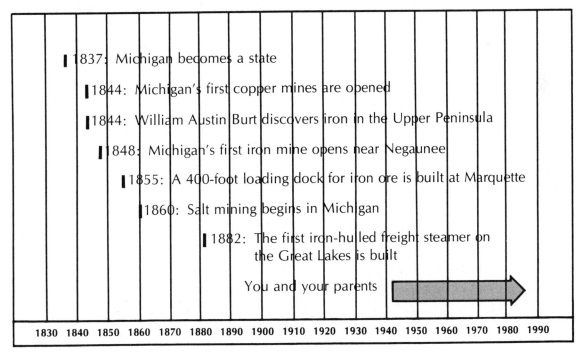

1837: Michigan becomes a state

1844: Michigan's first copper mines are opened

1844: William Austin Burt discovers iron in the Upper Peninsula

1848: Michigan's first iron mine opens near Negaunee

1855: A 400-foot loading dock for iron ore is built at Marquette

1860: Salt mining begins in Michigan

1882: The first iron-hulled freight steamer on the Great Lakes is built

You and your parents

1830 1840 1850 1860 1870 1880 1890 1900 1910 1920 1930 1940 1950 1960 1970 1980 1990

CHAPTER TEN
WEALTH BENEATH
THE GROUND

To the Indians it was a rock with a special spirit. To people who knew something about minerals, it was copper worth many dollars.

They called it the Ontonagon Boulder. The boulder helped start the copper boom. That boom changed the Upper Peninsula from a wilderness to one of the great mining areas of the United States.

In the late 1760s, when Michigan was part of the British empire, a white man named Alexander Henry heard the Indians talking about this boulder.

An Indian spread his hands almost four feet apart, saying, "It is this wide." Then he spread his hands a foot and a half or more apart to indicate its height. The Indian described the rock as red. Henry thought it might be made of copper.

A few years later, Henry paddled his big canoe along the shore of Lake Superior until he came to the mouth of the Ontonagon River at the western end of the Upper Peninsula. Paddling up the river, he found the boulder. It was as big as the Indian had said—much too big to move! It weighed about three tons.

In 1771, Henry and others began taking small amounts of copper from near the boulder. They could not get enough copper to make a profit, so they quit.

Fifty years went by before people again thought of mining Michigan's copper. In 1819 Governor Lewis Cass took his expedition past the boulder. A member of the

This drawing shows Lewis Cass visiting the three-ton Ontonagon Boulder in 1819. Julius Eldred moved the boulder to Lake Superior in 1843. From there it went to Detroit where it was claimed by the U.S. government. Today, it is in the Smithsonian Institution.

expedition, Henry Schoolcraft, wrote a report that made people start to think about copper again. Several tried to move the rock, but it was too big.

Then, Julius Eldred, of Detroit, decided to try. In 1841, he bought the boulder from the Indians. He and his men raised the rock on skids, but they could not move it. Finally, in 1843, they decided to try another method. They bought a small railroad car and built wooden railroad tracks.

The men pushed the car to the forward end of the tracks. Then they pulled up the back section of track and moved it to the front of the car. By continually moving the track sections and the car, they managed to transport the boulder 4½ miles to the main channel of the river.

From there they floated it on a barge to Lake Superior. And from there they moved it to Detroit by ship.

At Detroit, Eldred charged people twenty-five cents to see the boulder. But he did not get to keep the boulder. The U.S. government said Eldred did not own the boulder. It paid him for his expenses and moved the boulder to Washington, D.C.

The boulder finally came to rest at the Smithsonian Institution in the nation's capital. It is still there today.

MICHIGAN'S COPPER RUSH

One of the people who saw the Ontonagon Boulder while it was still in the Upper Peninsula was Douglass Houghton. In 1841, the year that Eldred bought the boulder, Houghton wrote a report about copper for the state legislature. He said there was plenty of copper. But he warned that the copper would be hard to mine.

Houghton's report got people excited. They dreamed of becoming rich quickly. Between 1844 and 1850 many journeyed to the Keweenaw Peninsula in search of the red metal. Most knew little about mining. They searched for pieces of copper and used picks and gunpowder blasts to loosen the rock. They did not become rich. At first the miners found only scattered bits of copper. In the summer they were bothered by black flies and mosquitoes. In the winter, the cold and snow sometimes seemed unbearable.

But the miners came, and soon firms began working on underground mines. Sometimes miners fought with each other. There were no policemen to keep them from doing this. Indians lived in the copper area, but there was no one to settle problems between miners and Indians.

One band of Chippewa Indians refused to let the miners use their land on Isle Royale. This frightened people, and in 1844, the federal government built Fort Wilkins at the tip of the Keweenaw Peninsula. The soldiers were not needed. The miners and the Indians solved their problems. In 1846, the soldiers left.

DEEP MINE SHAFTS

Between 1844 and 1850, twenty-four firms opened mines in the Copper Country. Only six were successful. One of the six was the Pittsburgh and Boston Mining Company.

Men entered early copper mines by ladders, which was dangerous. The copper was hauled up in buckets or big pieces.

The company's first mine produced little copper. So the company moved to a second place, near Eagle River. There it opened the Cliff Mine. For a while, the mine produced copper, but it was expensive. The mining shaft was 700 feet deep, and still very little copper was found.

The mine owners met to decide what to do. Some thought they should invest more money in the mine. But some said, "Not a penny more!"

One owner, Charles Avery, stood up and asked, "What about copper mining in Europe? How deep do they sink shafts over there? Does anyone know?"

None of the owners knew. But the mine superintendent, Edward Jennings, had the answer. He told the owners, "Seven hundred feet is no fair test for a shaft. Why, in Cornwall [England] we hardly ever find any copper above eight hundred feet."

Jenning's reply impressed Avery. Avery told the other owners, "I'll lend the company $60,000. Let's sink that shaft a few hundred feet more."

Avery's loan paid off. At deeper depths, great amounts of copper were mined. By 1870, the mine had earned more than $2 million. Meanwhile other mines were also successful. For forty years, from 1847 to 1887, Michigan led all other states in producing copper. In some years, it produced 90 percent of the nation's copper.

Copper mining greatly affected the economy of the Keweenaw Peninsula. Between the end of the Civil War (1865) and 1900, the population of Houghton County grew from 9,000 to 66,000. Only three counties in the state had more people than Houghton. The number of employees working for the most successful mining company, the Calumet and Hecla, grew from 4,000 to 21,000.

THE CORNISH HELP

People from Cornwall, in southwestern England, helped develop copper mining in the Upper Peninsula. The Cornish were known as the best underground hard-rock miners in the world. Many of them moved to Michigan for two reasons. First, the Cornwall copper and tin mines were producing less metal. Jobs were getting hard to find, and wages were low. Workers were

These men worked at the Cliff Mine near Eagle River. The Cliff was one of the Upper Peninsula's richest copper mines.

earning less money. Second, Michigan mines needed more workers.

In Michigan, the Cornish revolutionized mining. They changed how workers drilled and blasted. Many of them became foremen and managers of mines.

The Cornish also brought a special food to Michigan—pasties. To make pasties, meat and vegetables are wrapped in pie dough and then baked. In the mine, the pasties could be heated easily by "a Cornish stove"—a candle burning underneath a shovel.

The mines also attracted immigrants from Sweden, Finland, Norway, Ireland and other European countries.

PROBLEMS IN THE COPPER MINES

The mines were still bringing wealth to the Copper Country in the 1900s. But by then there were problems.

As the years went on, miners had to dig deeper and deeper to find copper in the Upper Peninsula. This was costly.

In the western part of the United States, copper was closer to the surface. This made mining easier and cheaper.

Michigan mining companies tried to make the miners work faster. They found a drill that could be used by one man instead of two. The miners did not like the new drill. They were afraid a man working alone could be more easily hurt in an accident. The miners also wanted higher wages and shorter working hours.

Some miners did not like living in company towns. In company towns, workers rented their homes from the company. The company owned the stores in town. It often built good schools, libraries, hospitals and churches for the town. But workers did not like the idea of having the company make all the decisions about how they lived.

The first time Michigan miners went on strike was in 1872. They stopped working to try to force the company to change. They and others who went on strike later were not very successful.

On June 22, 1913, many workers walked out of the copper mines and went on strike. They did not return until April 14, 1914. They won an 8-hour day and a minimum

Miners were upset when these two-man drills were replaced by one-man drills.

wage of $3.00 a day. They did not get the owners to say they could have a union.

In the middle of the strike, a tragedy occurred. The striking miners were having a Christmas party at Italian Hall in Calumet. Someone yelled, "Fire!" There was no fire, but in the rush to leave the building, 73 women and children were killed.

Many miners left the Copper Country because of that tragedy. Others left because the strike meant they had no money for food and housing. After the strike ended, copper production increased for a while. Then it began to decline. In 1970, there was only one copper mine left in Michigan.

THE IRON MINES

Iron was the other important Upper Peninsula metal. Railroads were built with iron. Iron ships were substituted for wooden ships on the Great Lakes and the

William Austin Burt (left) discovered iron in the Upper Peninsula. In 1844 he was surveying land. Suddenly the needle on his compass began swinging around wildly. Burt and his men searched for the cause and found pieces of iron ore. The magnetic pull of the iron was turning the needle in different directions. Soon iron was being mined at the Jackson Mine near Negaunee. The Jackson Mine (above), like most iron mines, was an open pit carved from the surface.

oceans. New factories and tall buildings were built using iron. From 1868 to 1900, Michigan was the nation's leading producer of iron.

BURT DISCOVERS IRON

On September 19, 1844, William Austin Burt was surveying in the Upper Peninsula. He was paid by the U.S. government. Burt and his crew were working near what is now Negaunee. They were marking the location of township borders.

The needle on the surveyor's compass began jumping around instead of pointing to the north. Burt told his crew to examine the area closely. They found numerous pieces of ore. Burt recognized the ore as iron. The magnetic pull of the iron was causing the needle to swing around.

A year after Burt's discovery, Philo Everett of Jackson went to the Upper Peninsula to search for a copper mining site. Instead he found iron ore. He and others founded the Jackson Iron Company.

The Jackson Company built a forge near Negaunee in 1847 and made its first iron in 1848. In nature, iron is mixed with other elements. At a forge, iron and limestone are heated by burning charcoal. When the iron melts, the other elements combine with the limestone and float to the top. The pure melted iron is drained onto sand. There it cools and becomes hard again. The cooled bars of iron are called pig iron.

MOVING THE IRON

The iron ore at Negaunee was easy to mine. It was lying all over the ground. But getting the pig iron to the lake was a slow process. There were neither railroads nor good roads. The iron could be moved to the lakeshore at Marquette only by sled during winter months.

In 1855 a plank road was built from Ishpeming to Marquette. That allowed wagons to be used all year. Two years later a railroad made things even easier. As new iron was discovered, more railroads had to be built.

At first, loading the iron onto ships was difficult. Men had to move wheelbarrows loaded with the iron onto ships. Then, in 1859, a high 400-foot long dock was built out into the lake at Marquette. Railroad cars crossed a high trestle to move onto the dock. There they dumped the iron into huge bins beneath the dock. The iron was then poured from the bins into the hatches of boats tied beside the dock.

BRIDGING THE RAPIDS

Once on board Great Lakes boats, the iron had one more hurdle to jump. At Sault Ste. Marie, the St. Marys River connects Lake Superior and Lake Huron.

Lake Superior is about nineteen feet higher than Lake Huron. So the river had rough rapids. Boats could not sail from one lake to the other. Men had to unload the iron from the boats, carry it by wagon along the shore and load it into other boats for the trip through the rest of the Great Lakes.

Michigan decided to build a canal where the rapids were. The canal included two locks to raise and lower boats. When a boat from Lake Superior moved into the lock, giant doors or gates were shut at each end of the lock. Then water was removed from

Before 1850, the rapids in the St. Marys River blocked the passage from Lake Superior to much lower Lake Huron. The first ship locks at Sault Ste. Marie were built in the 1850s to raise and lower the ships past the rapids.

the lock until the boat was at the same level as Lake Huron. The lower gate was then opened so the boat could go on its way. If the boat was bound upward, the opposite process applied. The gates were shut, and water was pumped into the lock until the ship reached the same level as Lake Superior.

Building the Soo Canal was difficult. The hardest part was blasting through one foot of solid granite. After two years of work, the locks and canal opened in 1855. Copper and iron could now be shipped easily to Chicago, Cleveland, Milwaukee, Detroit and other ports on the Great Lakes. Mine production increased.

The locks solved the problem of the rapids. The storms that cross the Great Lakes were not as easy to deal with. In 1847 the U.S. Congress approved the building of the first Lake Superior lighthouses at Whitefish Point and Copper Harbor. The lights helped sailors know where they were. They also warned them of dangerous places. In especially dangerous places, life-saving crews patrolled the shore looking for boats in trouble. Sometimes they were able to rescue the crews of such vessels.

150

One of the unusual ship designs on the Great Lakes was the whaleback. It allowed cargoes to shift during lake storms for better balance. The sides were rounded like a whale's sides. Whaleback ships were used mainly in the 1890s.

NEW BOATS

When the Soo Locks opened, wooden sailing boats carried the iron and copper. Steamboats were already carrying passengers, but not freight. Ship owners thought sailboats could carry freight at a lower cost than steamboats could.

But after the Civil War, both the sail and wooden boats began to disappear. Iron boats could be built longer and larger than wooden ones. They could carry more freight. And they were safer.

In 1882, the first iron-hulled freight steamer used on the Great Lakes, the *Onoko,* was built. The first Great Lakes boat made of steel, the *Spokane,* was launched in 1886.

Two years later, Alexander McDougall designed the "whaleback" expecially for the Great Lakes. It was strong and inexpensive. It allowed cargoes to shift to balance the boat during storms. By 1906, even these boats seemed old-fashioned. New boats had bigger hatches for faster loading. Some were 600 feet long.

Better ships meant less need for local furnaces. Iron ore could be carried to major cities before it was made into pig iron.

Communities built around furnaces began to fade away.

One example of this is Fayette, near Escanaba. In 1884 Fayette produced more pig iron than anyplace else in the Upper Peninsula. Five hundred people lived there. In 1891, Fayette stopped making pig iron. Soon no one lived there. Fayette had become a ghost town. Today the townsite has been partially restored and is operated by the Michigan Historical Museum.

Like copper mining, iron mining became more difficult in the twentieth century. The rich ore had been used up. Mines in other states, like Minnesota, produced better ore more cheaply.

MICHIGAN'S OTHER MINES

In 1841 Douglass Houghton reported traces of gold and silver in the Upper Peninsula. People who hoped to get rich quickly hurried north. But they found little gold or silver.

Later, miners found small amounts of both metals. And at one time, twelve gold mines operated in Marquette County. The largest was the Ropes near Ishpeming.

Salt turned out to be more valuable than gold or silver in Michigan. The salt was left behind when the ancient seas that once covered Michigan dried up.

The mining of salt for sale started in the Saginaw River Valley about 1860. The first salt was found in underground brine pools. After the brine, or salty water, was pumped to the surface, it was boiled. The moisture evaporated in the boiling process and left salt behind. Other salt was found as hard, **underground** rock.

People began mining salt beneath Detroit in 1910. The salt there is hard, allowing tunnels like these to be built.

In 1890 Michigan supplied half the nation's salt. It led the United States in salt production in all but four years between 1905 and 1958. There were three major salt areas—under the Detroit and St. Clair rivers, in the Ludington and Manistee area and in the Midland area.

Below Detroit, the salt is hard. Miners have gone down 1,200 feet to get the salt. Today, tunnels connecting the salt caverns are over 100 miles long. Nearly fifty million tons of salt have been taken from this mine. Experts say another thirty-five to seventy trillion tons of salt may be left there to mine.

152

Douglass Houghton was Michigan's first state geologist. His work revealed the Upper Peninsula's vast copper fields.

Only about 2 percent of the salt mined is used as table salt. The rest is used on winter roads, for meat packing and to make chemicals.

Herbert Henry Dow was the person who found a way to extract other chemicals from salt brine. His discovery allowed people to make chemicals used in drugs, photography, bleach and dyes, among other things. Today, the Dow Chemical Company, whose headquarters are in Midland, is one of the world's largest producers of chemicals.

Another important Michigan mineral was gypsum. It is used for making plaster, plaster board and insulating materials. People have been mining gypsum from under Grand Rapids since 1841. From 1901 to 1917, Michigan led the nation in producing gypsum.

Limestone was also left behind by the seas that once covered Michigan. Limestone is used to construct buildings and roads, make cement, refine iron ore into steel and manufacture paper, glass, leather, soaps and paints. The world's largest limestone quarry is found at Rogers City. It first opened for business in 1912.

CONCLUSION

After the Civil War, Michigan's economy depended on her natural resources—forests and minerals. People, mined copper, iron, a little gold and silver, salt, gypsum and limestone.

The iron and copper brought settlers to the Upper Peninsula. Mining also caused people to build railroads, new kinds of boats and the Soo Locks.

Michigan's economy was generally strong during this period. But not everyone was happy with the way things were done. In the next chapter, we will discover how some politicians and reformers tried to change things.

THE NEXT STORY

As this chapter begins, many people want to reform, or change, Michigan. Some think a few people have too much power over choosing who will run for governor or senator. Others think railroads and power companies have too many privileges. Some want more rights for women, workers or blacks. Some are worried about taking care of Michigan's fish and wildlife. Others think children should not work in factories. Still others want Michigan farmers to grow different crops.

PEOPLE

Governor **Hazen Pingree** wanted many reforms. He wanted railroads to pay the same taxes that other businesses paid.

Fred Warner, Chase Salmon Osborn and **Woodbridge N. Ferris** were all reform governors.

Lucinda Hinsdale Stone and **Anna Howard Shaw** led efforts to gain rights for women.

Caroline Bartlett Crane focused on cleanliness in meat processing plants.

PLACES

Farmers in **The Thumb**, around **Saginaw** and **Bay City**, began to specialize in sugar beets and beans. Those from **Traverse City** to **Benton Harbor** grew fruit. **Kalamazoo** was the center of the celery and mint industries.

WORDS

To **reform** something is to change it to make it better.

An **exemption** allows a person or company to not obey a rule.

Conservation means planning how something is used so that it is not wasted or destroyed.

Progressives were people from both the Democratic and Republican parties who wanted to reform many things. Progressive reforms included letting the public select political candidates in primaries, inspecting meat-packing plants, regulating utilities and ending child labor.

WHEN DID IT HAPPEN?

1837: Michigan becomes a state

1865: The Civil War ends

1869: The Michigan Supreme Court says that Detroit schools cannot separate children because of their race

1870: The University of Michigan accepts its first female student

1897: Hazen Pingree is elected governor of Michigan

1897: Michigan encourages people to grow sugar beets

1908: Michigan gets a new constitution

1921: The Conservation Commission is established

You and your parents

| 1830 | 1840 | 1850 | 1860 | 1870 | 1880 | 1890 | 1900 | 1910 | 1920 | 1930 | 1940 | 1950 | 1960 | 1970 | 1980 | 1990 |

CHAPTER ELEVEN
REFORMERS IN MICHIGAN

The year 1901 had just begun. Governor Hazen Pingree stood in front of the Michigan legislature. He was a large man with a well-trimmed gray beard. This was his last speech as governor of Michigan.

Pingree was not happy with the results of his four years in office. He was a reformer. But the senate had kept most of his reforms from passing.

One reform Pingree wanted was a tax on railroads. Years before, Michigan wanted companies to build railroads in the state. So it gave them special tax exemptions to lower their costs. The exemption allowed the railroads to not pay some taxes.

By 1897, when Pingree became governor, the railroads were making lots of money. They no longer needed special tax breaks. Pingree wanted them to be taxed like any other business.

First, Pingree convinced the Michigan House of Representatives to pass a railroad tax law. But the Michigan Senate defeated the bill. After Pingree was reelected in 1898, both the house and senate passed the tax bill. But the Michigan Supreme Court declared that the new law was not constitutional—it could not take effect.

Pingree next convinced people to change, or amend, the constitution. Now a railroad tax law would be constitutional. But the senate refused to act on the tax bill while Pingree was still governor.

This and many other things made Pingree angry. He called the legislators "parasites" who fed on state institutions. He said, "During the whole four years of my term as governor, I have only once been invited to the home of a single resident of the capital city of Michigan. Can you point to a place in the United States where a governor has been so treated by the citizens of a capital city?"

Kelly Nelson

EARLIER REFORMERS

Pingree was not the first person to want to reform, or change, Michigan. Since 1877, four other governors had tried and failed to have a fair tax on the railroads.

Some Michigan reformers were more successful. In 1869, for example, some people in Detroit challenged Detroit's segregation, or separation, of black and white school children. The group filed a lawsuit saying Joseph Workman's son, a black, should be allowed to attend a white school. The Michigan Supreme Court agreed. Detroit had to integrate its schools.

One of the men who supported Workman in the lawsuit was John Bagley. He became governor of Michigan in 1873. One of the women who supported Workman was Fannie Richards. In 1871 she became the first black teacher in Detroit's newly integrated school system.

Another group that wanted equality in education was women. In 1870 Lucinda Stone of Kalamazoo, led the fight to enroll the first woman, Madelon Stockwell, at the University of Michigan. Stone also began the women's department at Kalamazoo College.

Born in England in 1847, Anna Howard Shaw settled near Big Rapids with her family in the 1850s. Shaw graduated from Albion College in 1876. She studied to become a minister and was the first woman to become a minister in the Methodist Protestant Church. She also became a medical doctor. Shaw believed women should be able to vote. The right to vote is called suffrage. Shaw campaigned for woman's suffrage until it was won in 1919.

Hazen Pingree tried to reform Michigan laws. He was called a progressive.

PINGREE BECOMES A REFORMER

Pingree was not always a politician or a reformer. In 1889, he was a wealthy Detroit shoe manufacturer. His friends asked him to run for mayor as a Republican. They thought he would support things business people wanted. He did not. Instead, he insisted that taxes on factories be as high as those on homes. He lowered the rates charged for utilities—services such as water, gas and electricity that everyone needed. In 1893, he let people who had no work raise gardens on vacant city lots. To buy seed for their gardens, the mayor sold his own horse.

Pingree's old friends and many politicians did not like his reforms. But people who paid less for gas or streetcar rides supported him. In 1896, the Republican party needed a popular person to run for governor. Many thought Pingree could win. They were right.

Republicans in the state senate refused to pass most of Pingree's reforms. But the governor had won a lot of popular support for his ideas. Over the next fifteen years, many of his proposals would become law. In Michigan and throughout the United States, people who supported reforms like those proposed by Pingree would be called progressives.

THE PROGRESSIVE REFORMERS

Reform was especially popular between 1890 and 1917 because the way people lived had changed. Here are three examples of these changes.

In 1837, when Michigan became a state, everyone burned candles or kerosene lamps for light. Many stores sold candles and kerosene. By 1890, people in cities like Detroit used gaslights. One company provided all the gas in the town. It could charge anything it wanted to for its gas. In Detroit, gas was almost twice as expensive as in other cities.

In 1837, there were not many people in Michigan. Most were farmers. They knew each other and their government leaders. By 1890, there were many more people. Many lived in cities and worked in factories. They did not always know their

leaders. In some places, a few political leaders decided who would run for office. They were called bosses. These leaders sometimes paid poor people to vote a certain way. Other people sometimes gave money to the bosses to get special favors, like low taxes, from government workers.

In 1837, most people ate meat from animals they had raised and butchered themselves. By 1890, people in cities bought meat in stores. They did not know who had butchered (or slaughtered) the animals for their meat. The companies that provided this meat did not worry about how clean (or sanitary) their slaughterhouses were. They did not worry about diseases in the animals they butchered.

Some progressive reformers, like Governor Osborn, belonged to the Republican party. Others, like Woodbridge Ferris, were Democrats. All were concerned about these problems. They thought the government should keep gas companies from charging too much. They wanted to change the way political candidates were selected, so that bosses could not control elections. They wanted government to force slaughterhouses to be sanitary.

ECONOMIC REFORMS

Pingree's railroad tax was an economic reform to get rid of special privileges for businesses. It was passed in 1901, when Aaron Bliss was governor.

Another economic reform was government control of the prices utility companies charged for water, gas and electricity. In 1908 Michigan adopted a new constitution. Fred Warner was governor then. The new

Reformers in the late nineteenth century worked to clean up slaughterhouses. One reformer, Caroline Bartlett Crane of Kalamazoo (inset), visited slaughterhouses and told people about their filth. As a result, Michigan passed a meat inspection law in 1903.

constitution allowed cities to decide what their governments could do. They could decide, for example, to have their government regulate or own utilities.

SOCIAL REFORMS

Social reforms tried to make working and living conditions better. Many dealt with work in factories. The 1908 constitution allowed the legislature to pass laws about women and children who worked in factories. The legislature decided people under eighteen years old could work no more than 10 hours a day or 54 hours a

week. In 1912, it decided that companies should compensate (or pay) any workers who were hurt on the job. Until then, companies had no responsibility for workers injured while using dangerous machines.

Caroline Crane, of Kalamazoo, worked for another kind of social reform. In March 1902, she and members of Kalamazoo's Civic Improvement League visited seven slaughterhouses that sold meat to the city's markets. They found out that the slaughterhouses were very dirty.

"They were soaked with the rotten blood and filth of many years," they reported.

They noted that every exposed surface was coated and caked with blood, grime, grease, hair, mold and other filth. Worst of all, the women found the slaughterhouses were sending the meat from both healthy and sick animals to the markets.

Citizens were shocked when newspapers reported the group's findings. The Michigan legislature reacted. In 1903 it passed a meat inspection law. Crane was soon invited to investigate sanitation in other cities across the United States.

POLITICAL REFORMS

The progressives thought government should be more democratic and closer to the people. One way to do this was to let voters, instead of political bosses, decide who should run for office. This was done through a direct primary. This is an election in which all the members of a political party can vote to select the party's candidates for the final election. Michigan got its first workable direct primary law in 1909.

The referendum, initiative and recall were added to the Michigan constitution in 1913. A referendum allows voters to decide whether or not they approve of a law. An initiative lets voters introduce a new law. A recall vote lets voters remove an elected official from office. In each case, people sign petitions to have something voted on in a general election. Then the voters decide whether or not they want it.

AGRARIAN REFORMS

In 1900, farming was still Michigan's leading industry. Farmers wanted to control the rates railroads charged for shipping

Agrarian reforms included work to develop new crops like sugar beets.

their produce. They also worked to use science to grow more crops, run efficient farms and develop new crops. Some sent their children to the Michigan Agricultural College (MAC, now Michigan State University) to learn scientific farming. Some fought for what is now called home economics for their daughters. Some wanted the state to encourage new crops.

In 1897, Michigan decided to pay a penny for every pound of sugar produced from Michigan sugar beets. This bounty (or reward) did not last long. It was declared unconstitutional in 1900. However, the bounty and research at MAC were enough

161

Agrarian reformers were especially interested in the Michigan Agricultural College
(now Michigan State University). They believed that scientific methods could improve all parts of their lives from crops to
homemaking. The women above studied
home economics at the college. The men at
left worked in the fields to find new crops to
grow and better ways to grow existing
crops.

to start the beet sugar industry in Michigan. Soon beets were competing with beans as a leading crop in Michigan's Thumb region.

Other parts of Michigan also had special crops. People on the state's west side grew fruit. In the Benton Harbor-St. Joseph area, peaches were the leading crop. The Traverse City area was the nation's leading producer of tart cherries. In Michigan's southwest, celery, mint and onions were important crops.

As the forests were cut down, more people tried to farm in the northern Lower Peninsula and in the Upper Peninsula. Between 1900 and 1920, the number of farms in the Upper Peninsula doubled, from about 6,000 to 12,000.

Much of the northern land was not good for farming. Farmers who bought it soon had to sell it or leave it if no one would buy it. Some people believed that this land should be kept for forests and not for farmers. In 1899, the state created the Michigan Forestry Commission and began holding some of this land as state forests. But almost 30 years passed before the state had a broad program to save its forests.

CONSERVATION

By 1890 many reformers were worried about the loss of Michigan's natural resources. As chapter nine explained, lumbering destroyed much of Michigan's forests. Reforestation and forest fire prevention were both supported by progressives interested in conservation. Conservationists wanted to plan how forests, rivers and other natural resources were used so that they were not wasted or destroyed.

Fish hatcheries, like this one photographed in 1907, grew fish to replace those caught in Michigan's streams and rivers.

Conservationists worried about the loss of fish and game in Michigan. By 1900 there were no passenger pigeons or wild turkeys in Michigan. There were only a few grayling left in the Manistee River. Commercial fishing had decreased. Fishermen used fine nets that caught young as well as older fish. They took fish from the areas where they spawned other fish.

As early as 1865, Michigan passed a law that said fishermen had to use nets with larger holes so that young fish would not be

163

caught. But the state had no one to enforce the law, and people disobeyed it. The Fish Commission was formed in 1873. It established hatcheries to breed more new fish. But it was 1921 before the Conservation Commission was established. This commission provided the first effective protection of Michigan's forests and wildlife.

LIVING IN MICHIGAN IN 1900

As you have seen, reformers talked about what was wrong with Michigan and tried to change it. But there was also much that was right.

Michigan was growing. Industry, farming and mining were doing well. Towns and cities were growing.

At the time of statehood, in 1837, most new people came to Michigan from New England. Those who came from Europe were from Germany, England, Ireland, the Netherlands, Sweden and Canada. In 1900, newcomers were usually from other states of the Midwest. Most of the European immigrants were from Germany, Poland, Austria, Finland and Italy.

Some of the immigrants who came to Michigan between 1890 and 1910 became farmers, miners or lumbermen. Many found jobs in factories in the cities. Some lived in neighborhoods with other people from their homelands. Some began towns like the Yugoslavian community of Traunik in the Upper Peninsula. Others quickly became part of communities where people had different backgrounds.

As the newcomers came from all places, small towns grew. One sign of the growth of a town was its opera house. Starting in the 1870s, towns began building opera houses. They were not built just for opera. They were used for plays, other kinds of shows and community programs. There were no movies or TV then.

Tent shows came to town too. They were called chautauquas. A chautauqua was a traveling summer school. It was held out-of-doors or under a tent. There were lectures on history, reforms and international relations. There were concerts and plays. Most people did not travel a lot. For a few days each summer, the chautauquas brought the world to them.

People also got together for barn raisings or quilting bees. When a church or group needed to raise money, it often held a box social. Each young woman put a lunch for two in a box. She wrapped the box and tied it with ribbon and flowers to catch a young man's eye. Then the boxes were auctioned off. Each box went to the person who bid the most money for it. Each boy tried to guess which box his favorite girl had packed. The boy ate supper with the girl whose box he bought.

CONCLUSION

As the twentieth century began, Michigan was changing. Farming and industry continued to expand. Newcomers from foreign countries and other states helped cities grow rapidly. Some businesses and politicians had a great deal of power.

Reformers saw many things they did not like. Some wanted government to tax and treat all businesses the same. Some wanted rights for blacks, women or children who worked in factories. Some wanted more

Opera houses, like the Detroit Opera House above, were common attractions in many Michigan communities in the late nineteenth and early twentieth centuries.

decisions to be made by the voters. Others worried about sanitation or conservation.

Hazen Pingree was Michigan's first reform governor. He was not able to get many reforms into law, but he set the stage for later changes. The governors who followed Pingree were called progressives. They were part of a movement that included governors of other states and leaders of the United States.

The progressives enacted laws that form the basis of many laws today—laws about utilities, child labor, workmen's compensation, sanitary conditions and conservation. The initiative, referendum and recall were also progressive reforms.

Alpena

Gaylord

Muskegon

Saginaw

Grand Rapids

Flint

Lansing

Kalamazoo

Detroit

Adrian

Dowagiac

THE NEXT STORY

As this chapter begins, people are traveling in trains and horse-drawn carriages and wagons. By the time it ends, they are driving their own cars. Michigan is a leading industrial state. And the way Americans live has changed dramatically.

PEOPLE

Ransom E. Olds was Michigan's first successful automaker.

Henry Ford used the assembly line to build low-priced cars. For nineteen years, he offered only one kind of automobile—the Model T.

William Durant thought you needed to offer many kinds of automobiles to be successful. He founded the General Motors Company.

PLACES

Lansing was the home of Oldsmobiles.

Detroit was where Ford built his cars.

Flint was the home of the General Motors Company.

Adrian, Alpena, Gaylord, Grand Rapids, Kalamazoo, Muskegon, Saginaw, Dowagiac and many other towns had car companies for a few years.

WORDS

In an **internal combustion** or **gasoline-powered** engine, fuel is ignited by a spark plug to move pistons. In a steam engine, fuel heats water to make steam that moves the pistons. An internal combustion engine could be much smaller than a steam engine.

With an **assembly line** each worker stands in one place and adds one part to every car being made. Without an assembly line, a car stays in one place and workers bring the various parts to it.

WHEN DID IT HAPPEN?

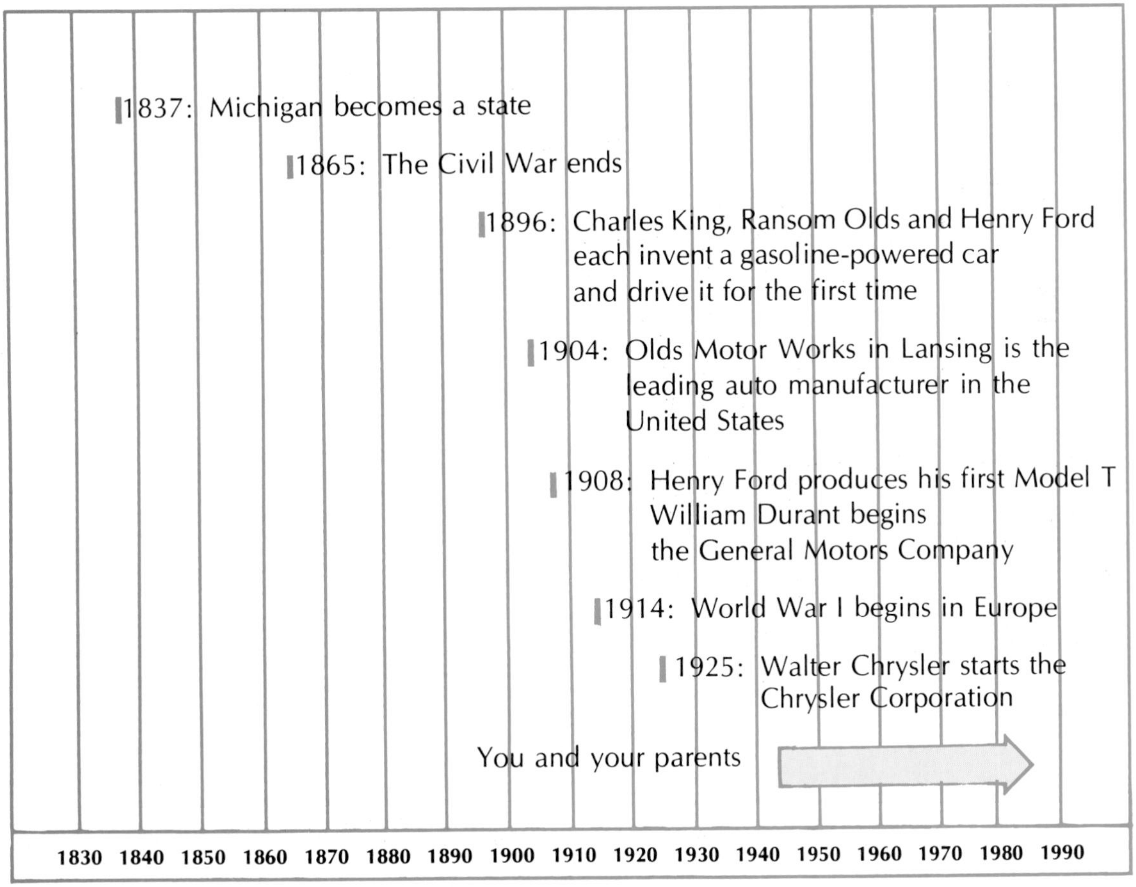

1837: Michigan becomes a state

1865: The Civil War ends

1896: Charles King, Ransom Olds and Henry Ford each invent a gasoline-powered car and drive it for the first time

1904: Olds Motor Works in Lansing is the leading auto manufacturer in the United States

1908: Henry Ford produces his first Model T
William Durant begins the General Motors Company

1914: World War I begins in Europe

1925: Walter Chrysler starts the Chrysler Corporation

You and your parents

1830 1840 1850 1860 1870 1880 1890 1900 1910 1920 1930 1940 1950 1960 1970 1980 1990

CHAPTER TWELVE
THE BIRTH OF THE AUTOMOBILE

Henry Ford was born in 1863. When he was a young man, people rode in carriages and wagons pulled by horses. There were no automobiles. One day in 1876, when Ford was only thirteen, he and his father rode in their wagon to Detroit. As their horses pulled them along, they came upon a big, steam-powered threshing machine. (A threshing machine separates grain from straw.) The boy made his father stop so he could look at it. He was amazed that a steam engine could move the thresher without horses. Ford began dreaming about a horseless carriage.

In the 1890s, in a shed behind his house, Ford started working on an engine. And in 1896 he invented his first car. Eventually he began the Ford Motor Company.

Many years later, on July 30, 1929, Ford's friends held a birthday party for him. One of the guests was a short, smiling man. He was Will Rogers, a famous humorist.

Rogers made a little speech about Henry Ford. Rogers said that no one had changed the lives and habits of Americans as much as Ford had. Then Rogers added, "Good luck, Henry. It will take us a hundred years to tell whether you have helped us or hurt us. But you certainly didn't leave us like you found us."

Indeed, the automobile changed both the way people lived and the way they worked.

THE FIRST CARS

Many people worked to invent the automobile. In 1886, a German inventor moved a vehicle using a gasoline engine. In the United States the first gasoline-powered car was driven in 1893 in Massachusetts.

Charles B. King drove Michigan's first gasoline-powered vehicle on March 6, 1896. He had built it in a machine shop. A local newspaper called it "a most unique machine."

The early cars were noisy. They clanged and banged along rough wagon paths. They scared horses that were pulling wagons and carriages. Between 1900 and 1910 at least fifty-seven small firms made some kind of auto in Michigan. Many plants were nothing more than large garages. And the cars were mostly experimental. Many were made by people who also made bicycles, carriages or wagons.

Cars were built in Adrian, Alpena, Chelsea, Constantine, Dundee, Gaylord, Grand Rapids, Hillsdale, Jackson, Jonesville, Kalamazoo, Marysville, Muskegon and Saginaw. Dowagiac had two car companies. The cars had many names—Roamer, Marquette, Earl, Hackett, Lion, Saxxon, Flanders, Brush, Hollier.

People called the cars "horseless carriages." One even had leather reins for the driver to use in guiding it. When the driver pulled suddenly·on the reins, the car stopped—just like a horse.

Most of the early automobile companies did not last long. The cars did not sell well. And people could not afford to keep making them. A few carmakers, however, were successful.

R. E. OLDS MAKES A RUNABOUT

The first Michigan person to successfully manufacture cars was Ransom E. Olds.

Olds moved to Lansing from Ohio in 1880. In 1886 and 1892 he tested vehicles powered by steam. But he saw a gasoline engine at the Columbian Exposition in Chicago in 1893. After that he began working on a gasoline-powered vehicle. He drove his first car on August 11, 1896. Olds then had to make his car run better, find people to finance building cars and locate a place to make them. In 1901 he set up a factory in Lansing.

At first, Olds made high-priced autos. In those early days most of the car owners were rich. Cars were expensive. They generally cost from one to three thousand dollars. Most people earned less than a thousand dollars a year.

The Olds Company lost money making high-priced cars. So Olds decided to make a small "runabout." The car would cost around $300 to build and sell for $650.

Before long his company was selling the Oldsmobile curved dash runabout. It was a simple vehicle. It looked like a carriage. It had no top to protect passengers from rain, snow and wind. It was steered by a tiller, or handle, that curved up from the floor.

By 1903, Olds was selling 4,000 cars a year. He was the first manufacturer in Michigan to produce cars in significant numbers. He also was one of the first to prove great profits could be made by producing a small, low-priced car.

His success led others in Michigan, including Henry Ford, to try to produce cars that could be sold in great numbers.

R. E. Olds was the first inventor to successfully make cars in Michigan. In 1907, he drove President Theodore Roosevelt (left rear) in a parade honoring the 50th anniversary of Michigan Agricultural College. Roy Chapin (right), an Olds employee, drove a curved dash Olds runabout to an auto show in New York City. It took him a week to get there.

In 1908, workers at the Olds Motor Works in Lansing posed for this photograph.

Henry Ford was the nation's best-known automaker. He built this car, his first one, in 1896. In 1903, after two earlier failures, he formed the Ford Motor Company.

HENRY FORD'S CAR

Henry Ford loved machines. He worked on steam engines and electric engines. Then, in 1893, like Olds, Ford saw a gasoline engine at the Columbian Exposition in Chicago. When he went back to Dearborn, Ford began working on a gasoline engine at night in a shed behind his home. During the day, he was an engineer for the Edison Illuminating Company.

Making a gasoline engine was not hard. Making one that would work in a small, moving vehicle was. Finally, on June 4, 1896, Ford drove his first car. It was early in the morning, before dawn, and Ford had to knock out the bricks around the door to get his car out of the shed. But the car ran for over a block. Ford was on his way.

On August 12, 1896, Ford went to hear a speech by a great inventor, Thomas Edison. Afterwards, Ford spoke with Edison. Ford asked if there was a future in the internal combustion (gasoline) engine. Ford later remembered that Edison pounded his fist on the table to emphasize his words. He told Ford, "Young man, that's the thing; you have it. Keep at it!"

Later Ford remembered that Edison's words encouraged him to work even harder. "Out of a clear sky," Ford said, "the greatest inventive genius in the world had given me complete approval."

Ford's most famous car was the Model T. For 19 years, the Model T was the only car made by the Ford Motor Company. By 1927 some 15 million had been produced.

Over the next few years, Ford formed several companies to back more experiments with his car and to produce cars. He formed the Ford Motor Company in 1903. But it was not until 1908 that he launched the car that made him famous—the Model T.

Ford and his engineers and mechanics had worked on plans for his new car for two years. Ford wanted a car that was "large enough for the family, but small enough for the individual to run and care for." It was to be "constructed of the best materials—by the best men to be hired—after the simplest designs that modern engineering can devise." It would be, he said, "so low in price that no man making a good salary will be unable to own one—and enjoy with his family the blessing of hours of pleasure in God's great open spaces."

Ford made the Model T and no other car for nineteen years. All of the fifteen million Model T's made were painted black. Ford would not allow any other color. American's called the Model T the "Tin Lizzie" because it rattled so much that people thought it was made of tin. The Tin Lizzie literally put America on wheels. It was cheap and dependable. Almost anyone could repair it using pliers and a screwdriver. In 1911, twenty percent of the automobiles produced in the United States were Model T's.

Ford was the first carmaker to use mass production techniques that made it possible to produce less expensive cars. He introduced a moving assembly line to save time and costs. As the car chassis moved on a track, parts were put on it.

HENRY FORD'S FACTORY

During the Model T's first six years, part of each car was assembled on a moving conveyor belt. But part of each car had to be assembled the old way. The car frame sat in one place while workers carried items to it. It took ten hours to assemble a car.

In 1914, Ford built a full assembly line at his Highland Park plant. The car no longer sat in one place. It kept moving along on a conveyor belt. As the body passed each worker, that worker fastened another part on the car. For instance, one worker did nothing but install steering wheels. Now it took only six hours to assemble a car. That year the Model T sold for $490. By 1916 the price of the Model T had dropped to $360.

Other people had used assembly lines to make things. But Henry Ford was the first to perfect this form of mass production for automobiles.

Ford's factories were efficient, but he still had trouble keeping workers. Everytime a

In 1908 William Durant formed the General Motors Company. In a few years, six other auto firms joined the company.

new worker came, the company lost money while it taught him how to do his job. There were many good jobs in Detroit, and workers changed jobs often to get better pay.

To keep workers longer, Ford introduced the idea of a minimum wage in the auto industry. In 1914, he announced that his company would pay at least $5.00 for an eight-hour day. This was twice the wage most workers earned. Ford also insisted that his workers live with families, dress in certain ways and not drink or smoke.

Ford thought he could make more money by paying workers well and keeping them longer. He was right.

GENERAL MOTORS IS BORN

Henry Ford thought the best way to succeed was to make one car well. William Durant of Flint thought it was better to offer customers many different kinds of cars. Both were very successful.

Durant made horse-drawn carriages in Flint. At first he did not like automobiles. In 1902 he told his daughter that she could not ride in a friend's car because it was too dangerous. But in 1904 Durant changed his mind. First he bought the Buick Motor Company.

Durant was not an inventor like Ford and Olds. He was good at advertising and selling cars. His company grew. In 1908 he formed the General Motors Company (GMC). Within a few years GMC owned not only Buick, but also Oldsmobile, Cadillac, Chevrolet, Pontiac and Fisher Body. Durant even tried to buy Henry Ford's company. But he and Ford could not agree on a deal.

Eventually GMC became the nation's largest carmaker.

THE SELF-STARTER

Others besides Olds, Durant and Ford helped Michigan become the automobile state. A key person was Charles Kettering. In 1911 he invented the electric self-starter. It was first used in 1912 Cadillacs.

Before that, to start the engine you stood in front of the car and turned a heavy crank. Kettering's self-starter made the automobile much easier to use. Anyone could sit in a car and start it easily. Few women had struggled with the cranks. With the self-starter, many more women began to drive.

MICHIGAN IS AMERICA'S CAR CAPITAL

By the time World War I began in Europe in 1914, Michigan was the automobile capital of the nation. Ford and General Motors were well established. They and smaller Michigan companies made over three-fourths of the cars in the United States. Detroit was the nation's fourth largest industrial city. (It had been the sixteenth largest in 1900.)

After the war, smaller companies continued to fail or be absorbed by larger ones. Walter Chrysler, who had worked for General Motors, took over two of these small companies. In 1925 he began making Chrysler, DeSoto and Plymouth cars. In 1928 he added the all-steel cars built by Horace and John Dodge. The third member of the "big three" car companies was now on its way.

A few smaller companies survived for many years. Packard earned a reputation as one of America's finest and most expensive cars. The company's slogan was "Ask the man who owns one." In 1912 the Essex, made by Hudson, became the first practical fully-enclosed automobile. Others that survived into the 1920s with large sales were the Overland, the Studebaker, the Oakland, the Hudson and the Reo.

MICHIGAN'S ADVANTAGES

It is easy to see why Michigan, and not Ohio or Illinois or somewhere else, was the

As early drivers learned, dirt roads handled horses well, but not cars.

place where people built cars. Several things existed together in Michigan.

1. Michigan had people who were manufacturing things like carriages. These people had skills and knowledge that could be used in experimenting with automobiles.
2. Michigan had people who had made a lot of money in mining and lumbering. Both of these industries were dying out. These people needed new places to invest their money. Some were willing to invest in factories to make cars.
3. Michigan had some unusual men who combined technical skill and new ideas for making cars with the ability to finance a business and sell automobiles.
4. Once Michigan firms became known for their cars, other people interested in making cars came to Michigan.

176

Most people used their cars to travel to new places or to get to work. But others were more inventive. This car was used to cut wood.

HOW THE CAR CHANGED AMERICA

Will Rogers said that Ford and the car "certainly didn't leave us like you found us." The car made it easier for people to move from place to place and that changed such things as these:

1. Life on the farm was not so lonely or isolated. In a buggy or wagon, a farmer had been able to cover only 20 miles or so a day. In an auto the farmer could quickly drive to town or a neighbor's house.

2. People did not have to live as close to their work. They began to move to suburbs and drive to work. As people moved from the center city, they eventually built shopping malls, drive-in restaurants and drive-in movies.

3. For entertainment, people drove to movies instead of staying home and reading books or playing games with the family.

4. People demanded better roads. Muddy, rutted roads were all right for horse-drawn wagons. But people with cars wanted straight, paved roads. They also needed highway maps.

5. People began driving to different places for summer vacations, instead of going to summer cottages or resort camps. Because people could travel, they were no longer as interested in traveling shows that came to them. Circuses, tent shows and carnivals became less popular.

6. Trucks and buses began to compete with trains to carry passengers and freight.

7. People preferred to drive their own cars instead of using mass transportation such as trolleys.

In the early days of the auto industry, automakers and auto dealers did many unusual things to call attention to their products. Here a Cadillac touring car is matched against a team of horses in a tug of war to see which is stronger.

The car indirectly caused other changes such as these:

1. Advertising signs and litter became as much a part of country scenery as green trees and plowed fields.
2. City streets were no longer filled with horse manure. They were cleaner and healthier. It would be many years before pollution from automobiles would be a problem.
3. Travel became dangerous. People who might otherwise be friendly often became discourteous, violent, reckless and selfish when they drove cars. In the first eighty years of automobile use in the United States, 2.5 million people died in accidents. This is twice as many as died in all the wars in this nation's history.
4. Automakers, especially Ford, demonstrated that manufacturers could make money by building products for average people. They sold large numbers of low-priced cars to the "mass market" instead of small numbers of high-priced cars to the "rich market." Other companies followed their lead.

These Olds Curved Dash Runabouts paraded in Lansing in 1900. Three years later, R. E. Olds was selling over 4,000 cars a year. That made him the nation's largest automaker. The horses and carriages in the background would soon fade from use.

5. Ford's moving assembly line worked so well that other industries adopted it. Workers saw only a small part of the product they made, but the products were much cheaper to buy.

6. New industries grew up to make parts needed for cars. Some examples were tires, spark plugs, valves, pistons, steel, oil and gasoline.

7. Service stations and garages were needed. So more jobs were created.

8. Inventors began using gasoline-powered engines for other machines. Ford, for example, built a gasoline-powered tractor.

CONCLUSION

Between 1896 and 1914 Michigan became the nation's auto capital. In 1929, Will Rogers asked whether Henry Ford helped us or hurt us by making the auto so popular. We may never be able to answer that with absolute certainty. But we can agree that Ford—along with Olds, Durant, Chrysler and others—changed the way we live and the way industry operates.

THE NEXT STORY

In this chapter cornflakes, streetcars and cement highways change Michigan. Some Michigan men go to Europe to fight in World War I. They hope the war will bring peace to the world forever, but it does not do this. The war speeds up changes like traveling by airplane, granting women the right to vote and prohibiting alcoholic drinks. One thing that does not change is the practice of racial segregation.

PEOPLE

Charles W. Post and **William K. Kellogg** made breakfast cereal in Battle Creek.

Governor **Alexander Groesbeck** wanted better roads in Michigan.

Charles Lindbergh was the first person to fly nonstop across the Atlantic Ocean.

Elijah McCoy was a well-known black Michigan inventor.

John C. Dancy was head of the Detroit Urban League from 1918 to 1960. The League tried to improve life for blacks.

Ossian Sweet and his family were black. They were attacked by a mob because they lived in a white neighborhood.

PLACES

Battle Creek became famous for its breakfast cereals.

Camp Custer was an Army training base during World War I.

Selfridge Field was built to train Army pilots.

Idlewild was a resort for black people.

WORDS

Streetcars, trolleys and **interurbans** were like modern buses, except that they ran on rails like trains.

Segregation means separation. In the United States between 1896 and 1954, it was legal to require blacks and whites to use separate hotels, schools and other public facilities. This is not legal today.

Things that laws say you can do are **legal**. Things laws say you cannot do are **illegal**. During **prohibition** it was illegal to sell alcoholic drinks such as beer.

WHEN DID IT HAPPEN?

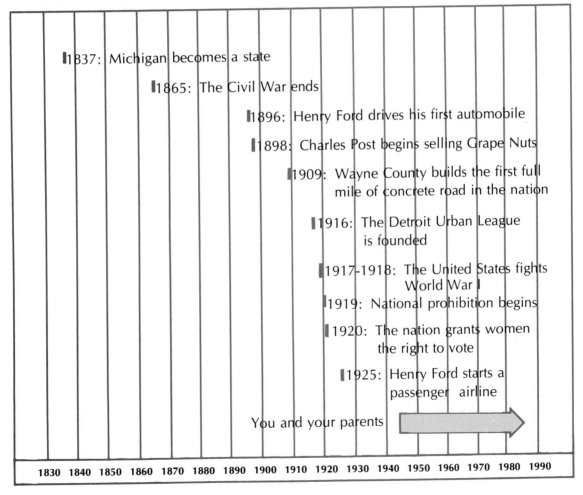

1837: Michigan becomes a state

1865: The Civil War ends

1896: Henry Ford drives his first automobile

1898: Charles Post begins selling Grape Nuts

1909: Wayne County builds the first full mile of concrete road in the nation

1916: The Detroit Urban League is founded

1917-1918: The United States fights World War I

1919: National prohibition begins

1920: The nation grants women the right to vote

1925: Henry Ford starts a passenger airline

You and your parents

| 1830 | 1840 | 1850 | 1860 | 1870 | 1880 | 1890 | 1900 | 1910 | 1920 | 1930 | 1940 | 1950 | 1960 | 1970 | 1980 | 1990 |

CHAPTER THIRTEEN
NEW MACHINES, IDEAS AND
A WAR CHANGE MICHIGAN

Charles W. Post did not have a lot of money. He had been an inventor and salesman. As an inventor, he once used 150 sticks of dynamite to try to make it rain. He fastened the dynamite to kites and flew the kites near some clouds. But when the dynamite exploded, no rain fell.

In the 1890s Post was in poor health. He decided to go to the health institute or sanitarium in Battle Creek for treatment.

The sanitarium was run by Dr. John Harvey Kellogg. The doctor thought Americans ate too much meat, eggs and potatoes for breakfast. So he toasted oats, wheat and corn to make cereals for his patients. His first cereal, Granola, was made of ground, toasted wheat and served with milk. Kellogg sold his cereals by mail to former patients, but he did not try to build a big, national cereal business.

Post was impressed with the food at the sanitarium. He thought he could sell some of it to the general public. Post started with the substitute for coffee that Kellogg had served. In 1896 he began making his own substitute coffee. He called it Postum.

Two years later he started making a cereal similar to the cereal he had eaten at the sanitarium. He called it Grape Nuts.

Post realized he could not make big

In 1896 Charles Post began making dry breakfast cereal in Battle Creek. The city soon became the breakfast cereal capital.

profits unless people knew about Postum and Grape Nuts. So he spent his profits on advertising. In advertisements, or ads, you tell people about your product or service and how good it is. You hope to make more people want to buy it.

In one ad, Post told women that Grape Nuts would make them more beautiful. Those kinds of ads worked. Soon, many people were buying Grape Nuts and Post was making a lot of money. Before long, he became a millionaire.

Meanwhile, William (Will) K. Kellogg was working on his own breakfast cereal.

Will was the brother of John Harvey Kellogg, the doctor who ran the Battle Creek sanitarium. Will helped his brother develop cereal for the sanitarium's patients. Then, in 1906, Will left the sanitarium and formed his own cereal company.

One of Will Kellogg's first products was Toasted Corn Flakes. Like Post, Kellogg advertised well. In one of his ads, he told housewives to go to their grocery store and ask the grocer to put Kellogg cereals on the store's shelves.

Before long, Kellogg also was a millionaire. The success of Post and Kellogg led others to start cereal companies in Battle Creek. They made cereals that had names like Try-a-Bita and Malta-Vita. But these companies did not succeed like Post and Kellogg. Battle Creek soon became known as the cereal capital of the nation. And Post and Kellogg were the nation's two leading makers of breakfast food.

RAILROADS HIT THEIR PEAK

As Post and Kellogg changed the way Michiganians and Americans ate breakfast, trolley cars and paved roads changed the way Michiganians went to work or play.

Between the Civil War and 1890, railroad trains faced little competition as they carried people and freight from town to town. Wagons pulled by horses or oxen were much slower than trains, and boats could not reach many towns. The trains stopped at villages and towns of all sizes several times a day.

In Michigan, trains first came to Mackinaw City at the tip of the Lower Peninsula in 1881. And in 1887, it became possible to travel from one end of the Upper Peninsula to the other by train. By 1910 there were about nine thousand miles of railroad track in Michigan. That was the most railroad mileage Michigan would ever have.

BOATS GET BIGGER

In Michigan towns along the Great Lakes, boats were as important as trains. These boats seemed to get larger every year. In 1904 the largest boat could carry 10,000 tons of iron ore. By 1930, the largest Great Lakes boat carried 15,000 tons of ore.

The bigger boats needed bigger locks at Sault Ste. Marie. In 1914, the United States built a lock there that was 1,350 feet long. The big boats also needed to load quickly. In 1913, Marquette built its first all cement and steel "pocket" docks on the shore of Lake Superior. The larger, stronger bins, or pockets, for holding the iron ore meant that boats could be loaded quickly.

STREETCARS AND INTERURBANS

When boats, trains and horse-drawn wagons were the main forms of transportation, people lived near their jobs. There was no way to quickly travel across town or to a nearby town everyday. Streetcars, interurbans and eventually paved streets and highways changed that. They provided inexpensive, reliable transportation. Using them, people could live in the suburbs several miles from their offices. They might even live in one town and work in another.

Streetcars and interurbans ran on tracks like trains. The first streetcars were pulled by horses. Then, in 1886, Port Huron became the first Michigan city to use electric-

Streetcars gave people convenient, low-cost travel. Electricity from overhead wires furnished inexpensive power.

ity to power its streetcars. The electricity ran through a wire above the track. A trolley wheel ran along the wire, picking up the electricity and sending it down a pole into the car. The cars were called trolleys.

Trolleys that carried passengers from one city to another were called interurbans. The first interurban in Michigan began running between Ypsilanti and Ann Arbor in 1891. It charged 10 cents a ride. The train charged 25 cents for the same trip. Soon 600 people were riding the interurban every day. The train had carried only about 40 passengers a day. By 1919, there were over 1,000 miles of interurban track in Michigan.

185

ROADS FOR MICHIGAN

Interurbans did not last long. They were soon challenged by cars and buses. These did not need tracks. They could go anywhere there was a road. At first though, there were not many good roads.

Michigan created a State Highway Department in 1905. In 1909 the Wayne County Road Commission paved Woodward Avenue in Detroit from Six Mile to Seven Mile Road. This was the first full mile of concrete road in the nation.

To make it easy for cars to travel, Michigan's roads needed to be smoothed out and covered with clay, gravel or pavement.

Some areas tried to do this using volunteer help. For example, on June 9, 1913, about 5,000 volunteers in eight counties on the shore of Lake Huron held a road-building bee. By nightfall the men had covered many soft dirt roads with clay and put gravel on some roads. Later, Governor Woodbridge Ferris set aside two days for a statewide road-building bee. Men all over the state volunteered.

While these bees helped, they did not begin to provide enough good roads. Automakers and auto owners pushed for help from government. In 1916, the federal government voted to spend $180 million for new roads during the next five years.

In 1919, Michigan voters approved a constitutional amendment to help road building. It allowed the state to borrow $50 million for a highway building fund. The money went to local communities. There was still no state highway system.

Alexander Groesbeck was governor of Michigan from 1921 to 1927. He liked

Governor Alexander Groesbeck began Michigan's statewide network of roads.

well-organized things. He reorganized state government. Then he began working on a statewide system of roads. In 1925 he agreed to a tax on gasoline to pay for the roads. He pushed for wider roads and concrete roads. The state roads went around some towns instead of through them, so that people could travel faster.

Where roads could not go, Groesbeck found other solutions. Under his leadership, Michigan began running ferry boats that carried cars across the Straits of Mackinac. The ferries linked the two peninsulas until the Mackinac Bridge opened in 1957.

Good roads let people travel farther to work. They also let them travel great dis-

Like most Michigan roads, Detroit's Woodward Avenue often became too muddy for cars (top). In 1908 it received the nation's first mile of concrete highway (bottom).

tances for vacations. Before cars and roads, most people waited for a traveling show to visit town or went to one place every summer for vacation. With cars and roads, a family might go to Chicago one year and New York the next.

WORLD WAR I

In 1914, countries in Europe began to fight what became known as World War I. The United States did not enter that war until April 6, 1917. The war showed a good and a bad side of people in Michigan and throughout the United States.

Germany and Austria were the enemies of the United States in the war. Michigan's bad side showed when it treated its 80,000 German and 20,000 Austrian immigrants as if they were enemies too.

Hamburger, named after a German town, became "liberty sausage." Frankfurters, also named for a German town, became "hot dogs." Schools stopped teaching German. German music became unpopular. Germans who did not support all efforts to raise money for the war often found yellow paint smeared on their homes.

On the positive side, Michigan people organized quickly to support the war. Automobile factories began making army trucks, airplane engines and tanks. The furniture factories in Grand Rapids made airplanes. Farmers and iron and copper miners produced more. People everywhere ate less meat and used less fuel so that more could be sent to the soldiers.

Some 175,000 Michigan men served in the army during World War I. About 5,000 of them died and about 15,000 were wounded. To train new soldiers, the United States set up thirty-two centers across the nation. One was built west of Battle Creek. It was called Camp Custer. Almost overnight, farm families were moved out of the area. Then 2,000 construction workers moved in. In about seven weeks the workers built more than two hundred wooden buildings. Eventually the camp had 3,000 buildings. Thousands of soldiers from Michigan and Wisconsin trained there.

The Army also built airfields to train pilots. One was Selfridge Field near Mt. Clemens. It opened in 1917. The country's first school of aerial gunnery was there. Among those trained at Selfridge was America's most famous pilot of the war, Eddie Rickenbacker.

The war ended in 1918. After the war Michigan life continued to change. The changes were not caused only by the war. But the war speeded them up. Three big changes were in the use of airplanes, the adoption of prohibition and the advance of women's rights.

FLYING

World War I allowed many people to learn to fly. It gave others new ideas about what airplanes could do.

In 1922, in Detroit, William Stout made the first all-metal passenger plane in the nation. It carried eight passengers. The metal was much stronger than the wood and cloth used on earlier planes.

Soon Stout and Henry Ford joined forces. Ford built an airport in Dearborn. There they produced the Ford Tri-Motor plane. Pilots called it the "Tin Goose." It was so dependable that Ford Tri-Motors were flying for many years afterwards.

In 1925, Ford aircraft began flying on a regular schedule from the Dearborn airport to Chicago and Cleveland. Ford claimed it was the first regularly scheduled airline service in the nation. He was proud that in 1925 not a single accident or a day's interruption of service occurred.

Charles Lindbergh was born in Detroit in 1902. In 1927 he became the first person to fly nonstop across the North Atlantic. He flew alone in a small single-engine airplane. After Lindbergh took off from New York, millions listened to another new invention, the radio, to learn his fate. When he landed in Paris, the whole nation celebrated. (One of the first commercial radio stations in the nation was Detroit's WWJ. Its first broadcast was in 1920.)

PROHIBITION

One big change after World War I was called prohibition. Under prohibition it was illegal to sell alcoholic drinks like beer and whiskey. Various people had talked about outlawing liquor for almost 100 years. They did a good job of teaching other people about the bad effects of liquor.

In 1916, the majority of the voters in Michigan agreed to prohibit the sale of liquor in the state. They thought this was

Many Michigan men received training at Battle Creek's Camp Custer (top left and above) during World War I. The postwar attraction with airplanes led Detroit native Charles Lindbergh (top right) to make the first solo flight across the Atlantic Ocean in 1927.

morally right. They also believed people who did not drink would work harder at their jobs. The law went into effect in 1918. A year later, the nation adopted a similar law by passing the Eighteenth Amendment to the Constitution.

But it was hard to make everyone stop drinking. People made beer and wine at home. Alcoholic drinks were legal in Canada. Some people brought large amounts of liquor from Canada to sell illegally in the United States. Much of this smuggling took place along the Detroit River. By the 1930s many people were convinced that prohibition could not work. They voted to end it. Prohibition was repealed, or ended, in 1933.

WOMEN'S RIGHTS

Before World War I, many women had begun to support themselves by operating new machines including typewriters and telephone switchboards. During the war, many men left their jobs to become soldiers and women replaced them. The more women worked outside their homes, the more unfair it seemed to not allow them to vote.

In 1919 Michigan's male voters gave women some voting rights. One year later, the nation adopted the Nineteenth Amendment to the U.S. Constitution. That amendment gave every woman in the nation exactly the same voting rights as men.

Michigan's first female state senator was elected in 1921. She was Eva Hamilton of Grand Rapids. Michigan's first female state representative, Cora Anderson of L'Anse, was elected in 1925.

One year after women won the right to vote, Eva Hamilton of Grand Rapids became Michigan's first female state senator.

Women changed the way they lived in other ways too. New machines made housework, such as laundry, easier. Women began to wear short skirts instead of ankle-length dresses. Some began to smoke cigarettes in public. Some cut their hair short. They felt freer to do what they wanted to do instead of what society told them to do.

SEGREGATION

One thing that did not change between 1900 and 1930 was segregation. Segregation was the practice of separating black and white people.

During the early twentieth century, blacks were barred from white resorts. Instead many stayed at Idlewild, a black resort community in Lake County near Baldwin.

One of the popular attractions at Idlewild was the Club House. Here resorters could purchase meals or meet and talk with others staying at Idlewild.

Segregation kept blacks and whites separate at Camp Custer during World War I (left). But it did not prevent the success of blacks such as inventor Elijah McCoy (right).

Black and white soldiers both fought for the United States in World War I. But blacks were kept together in all-Negro units. At Camp Custer, there were separate barracks for black soldiers.

Many black people fought segregation and some were successful in spite of it. For example, Elijah McCoy, who lived in Ypsilanti, was a mechanical engineer. Because he was black, he could not get a job in this field. Instead he became a fireman for the Michigan Central Railroad. He invented a device to automatically oil, or lubricate, the machinery he used. Soon railroads and steamships across the nation were using McCoy's lubricators.

Later, McCoy moved to Detroit. Eventually, he had his own company. He invented 78 different things during his lifetime.

Black people were not allowed to stay at white hotels or resorts. So they began to go to black resorts. One of the best-known black resorts was Idlewild in Lake County, Michigan. Black people from all over North America bought or rented lots and cabins at Idlewild. At first people stayed in tents and small cabins. Eventually, there were also nightclubs where people like Sammy Davis, Jr., and Aretha Franklin entertained.

In 1916 the Detroit Urban League was formed. Its goal was to improve life for black people in Detroit. From 1918 to

192

John Dancy, above with his wife Malinda, directed the Detroit Urban League.

1960, John Dancy headed the league. Under his leadership, the league ran a camp for black children at Grass Lake near Jackson. It worked for better jobs and housing for black people. In 1919 it set up a baby clinic so that black mothers could learn more about taking care of their children. To provide recreational facilities for blacks, it created a community center.

As industry grew in southern Michigan, more blacks came to work in the factories. In 1900, about 16,000 blacks lived in Michigan. By 1930, over 169,000 lived here. As more blacks moved to urban areas, tension between blacks and whites increased.

Some white people did not want blacks to live near them. Ossian Sweet was a black doctor. His family moved into a white neighborhood in 1925. A mob of white people gathered outside his house and began throwing rocks at it. Someone inside the house fired a gun at the mob. Two white men were killed. Dr. Sweet and members of his family were tried for murder. The jury decided the Sweets were not guilty because they had a right to defend their house. The case showed that minorities were protected by the law, but it did not change the attitudes of the people who supported segregation.

CONCLUSION

Between 1900 and 1929 people in Michigan got their first taste of many things that we take for granted today. These included breakfast cereals, good roads, airplanes, radios and voting rights for women.

Some of the changes made life easier. Some changes, like prohibition, did not work well and were ended. Some things, like racial segregation, did not change.

World War I made some of the changes happen faster.

In the 1920s business grew fast. People were optimistic about the future. They expected to earn more money every year. They expected everyone to own a car. Many borrowed and spent too much money. It was as if they were all blowing up a big balloon filled with hopes for the future. In the next chapter, we will talk about what happened when that balloon was broken by the Great Depression.

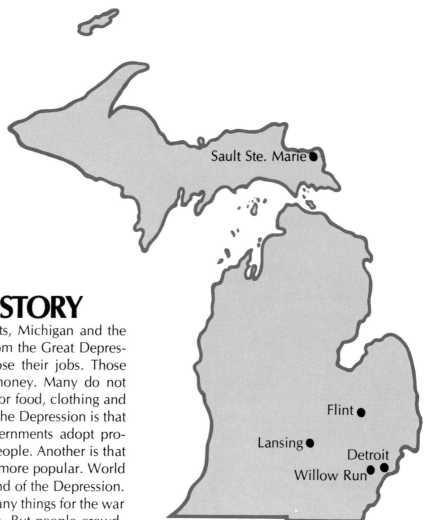

THE NEXT STORY

As this chapter starts, Michigan and the world are suffering from the Great Depression. Many people lose their jobs. Those with jobs earn less money. Many do not have enough money for food, clothing and homes. One result of the Depression is that federal and state governments adopt programs to help these people. Another is that labor unions become more popular. World War II comes at the end of the Depression. Michigan produces many things for the war and has plenty of jobs. But people crowding into cities to work in factories cause new problems.

PEOPLE

Franklin D. Roosevelt was president of the United States during the Depression.

Frank Murphy was governor of Michigan during the Flint sit-down strike.

Arthur Vandenburg was a United States senator from Michigan who helped plan for peace after the war.

PLACES

Flint was the site of an important strike.

Willow Run was the location of a large factory that was built to make B-24 bombers during World War II.

WORDS

During a **depression** prices and wages fall. People have less money, so they buy fewer things. Because fewer things are sold, there are fewer jobs.

A **labor union** is a group of workers who unite to bargain with the people they work for.

In a **sit-down strike,** laborers refuse to work but stay inside the factory so that the company can not bring in other people to do the work.

Under **rationing**, each person could buy only a limited amount of food or gasoline.

WHEN DID IT HAPPEN?

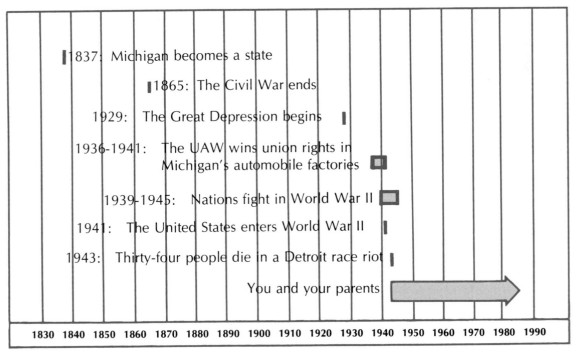

1837: Michigan becomes a state

1865: The Civil War ends

1929: The Great Depression begins

1936-1941: The UAW wins union rights in Michigan's automobile factories

1939-1945: Nations fight in World War II

1941: The United States enters World War II

1943: Thirty-four people die in a Detroit race riot

You and your parents

1830 1840 1850 1860 1870 1880 1890 1900 1910 1920 1930 1940 1950 1960 1970 1980 1990

CHAPTER FOURTEEN
THE GREAT DEPRESSION
AND THE GREAT WAR

Ann was in the first grade. For weeks she had looked forward to marching in her school's May Procession. The evening procession would end with the crowning of the Virgin Mary in church.

Then, on the morning of the procession, Ann's teacher announced that only girls who had white dresses and white shoes could march.

Ann had a white dress, but no white shoes. She knew her parents could not afford to buy her white shoes. They had no spare money. The nation was in the midst of the Great Depression. Ann tearfully decided she would just watch the procession. But her dad had a better idea. He found some paint and painted Ann's old black shoes white.

That evening, as Ann marched in the procession, she thought, "No one is prouder than I am."

The Great Depression was filled with stories like Ann's. People found new ways to help each other and solve problems. Bernice Boven's mother dyed flour sacks pretty colors and used them to make dresses for her daughters. Mrs. Dare Bryant's father took care of a neighbor's cow in return for two quarts of milk a day. Willard J. Prentice remembers that one Detroit restaurant owner, Speros Sassalos, fed University of Detroit students even if they could not pay until later.

There were also people who could not make ends meet. Some children went to bed hungry. Some families lost their homes.

Kelly Nelson

THE GREAT DEPRESSION

Many things combined to cause the Great Depression. For example, several years of dry weather meant that many farmers lost their crops. Another cause was people buying too many things on installment plans or on credit. In the 1920s people expected to earn more money every year. They bought things by paying only part of the price at first and promising to pay the rest later. The later payments were called installments. People bought cars, homes and businesses this way.

In 1929, prices and wages started to fall. People could not make their payments or buy new things. Stores sold fewer products, and factories made fewer products. Fewer workers were needed in stores and factories. Many people lost their jobs. The unemployed people could not pay their debts or buy new things.

One of the first things people stopped buying was cars. The Depression came quickly to Michigan because so many auto workers in Michigan were unemployed.

As industry slowed down, no one needed copper or iron from the mines in the Upper Peninsula. Many mines closed for several years. By 1933, two-thirds of the families in Keweenaw County needed some kind of relief or help. In the 1920s, some banks had loaned too much money to people. The banks lost this money when people could not pay their debts in the 1930s. Nearly 200 Michigan banks lost so much money that they had to go out of business. When these banks closed their doors, their customers lost the money they had in savings and checking accounts.

Detroit Mayor Frank Murphy led the city's Depression relief efforts.

HELPING THE UNEMPLOYED

At the beginning of the Depression, local government and charities were expected to take care of the poor. The state and federal governments had no major welfare programs. Most people believed that only workers who were lazy could not find jobs.

At first, local groups tried to deal with the Depression. In Flint, for example, the Methodist Church fed as many as 1,200 people a day. The Flint Community Fund raised money to help the needy. The Flint Lions Club gave free milk to 2,500 school children.

In Detroit, the city government, led by Mayor Frank Murphy, fixed up an abandoned warehouse so that homeless people could sleep there. At fire stations, firemen served food to the jobless.

One of the New Deal's better-known programs was the Works Progress Administration (WPA). WPA workers did many jobs. Above they repair a Detroit street in 1936.

As more and more people lost their jobs, two things became apparent.

1. Local government and charities could not care for everyone needing help.
2. Good, hard-working people often could not find jobs.

THE NEW DEAL

One man who thought that the Depression was so big that the federal government needed to help was Franklin D. Roosevelt. Roosevelt became president of the United States in 1933.

President Roosevelt called his programs the New Deal. Some of his programs—like insurance for savings accounts in banks— tried to help make sure another depression would not happen. Other programs tried to help the poor and the unemployed.

The New Deal program designed to help unemployed young men was the Civilian Conservation Corps, or CCC. The CCC provided camps for men 17 to 25 years of age. There were 103 camps in Michigan. Former army officers ran the camps. Each young man received thirty dollars a month in addition to food, bed and medical aid.

The CCC men did many important things. They constructed hundreds of miles of foot trails and roads. They planted thousands of acres of tree seedlings to replace the forests cut down by lumbering companies. They fought forest fires. They built firebreaks, fish hatcheries, picnic grounds, campgrounds, bridges and parks that are still enjoyed by people in Michigan. Most importantly, they worked and earned some money.

New Deal Programs to employ the jobless included the Civilian Conservation Corps (CCC). Besides replanting forests, the CCC built forest firebreaks (above).

Other federal agencies, such as the Works Progress Administration (WPA), gave jobs to artists, writers, laborers and craftsmen. These people painted murals for post offices, repaired streets and built park roads and buildings.

Many Depression programs are still part of our lives. They include:

1. Money payments for a person temporarily out of a job;
2. Social Security payments for retired people (during their working years, these people and their employers contribute to the Social Security system);
3. The state program to help unemployed people find jobs; and
4. The Federal Deposit Insurance Corporation, which insures bank deposits up to a certain amount.

THE LABOR UNIONS

Workers in Michigan had been joining together in unions since at least the 1830s. The purpose of the unions was to get better pay and working conditions for the workers. When a union could not get what it wanted, its members sometimes stopped working. This was called a strike. Often a company simply found new workers to replace the ones who were on strike.

At first, unions were organized around the jobs of skilled workers. These were called craft unions. Railroad engineers and railroad firemen belonged to different unions.

When the Great Depression began, very few people who worked in big factories belonged to unions. People who built cars did not have special skills that fit with the old craft unions. The auto workers were

The Michigan National Guard kept order during the Flint Sit-Down Strike.

paid well. Many had come from farms and did not know much about unions.

The Depression changed all of that. Wages fell. People were asked to work harder for less money. Workers who still had jobs were afraid of losing them.

The unions changed too. Workers in large factories saw the need to join unions. They began organizing by industry instead of by the kind of jobs they did. Everyone who built automobiles was urged to join the United Automobile Workers, or UAW. The unions organized by industry eventually formed the Congress of Industrial Organizations (CIO). Those organized by craft or job were part of the American Federation of Labor (AFL).

Laws also changed. For the first time, the government said that workers had a right to form unions. It said unions could negotiate with employers to get better wages and working conditions.

FLINT'S SIT-DOWN STRIKE

By 1936, the UAW had many members in the factories that belonged to General Motors (GM). GM agreed to bargain with the UAW, but it said it would also bargain with other unions.

On December 30 workers at Flint's Fisher Body Plant Number One heard a rumor that their work was going to be moved to a plant where fewer workers belonged to the UAW.

The Flint workers decided to go on strike. But they did not leave the factory. They stayed inside the factory so new workers could not be hired to replace them. This was called a sit-down strike. While it lasted, some workers ate and slept in the factory. Other union members stayed outside the factory. They carried signs, or pickets, stating their position. They also took food and supplies to the people in the factory. Soon the strike spread to other GM factories.

On January 11, 1937, the thermometer in Flint showed 16 degrees above zero. Shortly after noon, the company turned off the heat in one of the factories occupied by the strikers. Company police also removed a 22-foot ladder the UAW was using to get food and supplies to the strikers.

Some union members tried to take food through the gate to the strikers. But for the first time company police barred the way.

About 8:30 P.M. union organizer Victor Reuther arrived in a truck with a loudspeaker on top. He directed the people who were outside the factory and talked to the men inside. Soon the police and the strikers were fighting each other. Sixteen people were hurt, but no one was killed.

Frank Murphy was the governor of Michigan. He went to Flint and met with people from the union, the company and the city. They agreed that National Guard soldiers should go to Flint to keep more fights from happening. Murphy made it clear that the soldiers would not try to end the strike.

While the soldiers kept order, Murphy tried to get the union and the company to reach an agreement. They finally did so, and the strike ended on February 11. GM agreed to let the UAW be the only union it would bargain with for six months. This made it easier for the union to get more members. GM also agreed to stop trying to keep workers from joining the UAW.

THE UAW GROWS

The Flint sit-down strike proved that the UAW could win strikes. It became easier for it to get more members.

Still it took a long time for all the carmakers to agree to work with the UAW. Henry Ford believed he treated his workers well. He saw the unions as outsiders and fought hard against them. He fired people who joined them. He hired men who threatened workers who wanted to join the union. On May 26, 1937, these men beat up union organizers outside one Ford plant.

Finally, in 1941, the courts forced Ford to let the workers in his factories select a union to represent them. They chose the UAW. Michigan's era of labor violence was

At meetings, like the one advertised in this poster, union organizers urged auto workers to join newly-formed unions.

over. Michigan soon became a state with one of the most powerful labor organizations in the United States.

Three of the UAW leaders were Walter, Roy and Victor Reuther. The Reuther brothers had come from West Virginia to work in Detroit's auto factories. Victor led the Flint strike, and Walter was one of the people beaten up at the Ford plant. In 1946 Walter became president of the UAW. He became president of the CIO in 1952.

WORLD WAR II BEGINS

By the time the UAW won the right to represent Ford workers in May 1941, many Michigan factories were making guns, tanks, airplanes and other supplies for the countries fighting in World War II. The British Empire and the Soviet Union were fighting Germany and Italy. The war had begun in 1939. By 1941, Germany controlled most of Europe, including France. The United States was not yet in the war. However, it was making supplies for the British.

In November 1940, the Chrysler Corporation began work on a tank factory near Detroit. Its first tanks were shipped in September 1941. In April 1941 an even bigger project began at Willow Run near Ypsilanti. There, Henry Ford started building a plant to make Liberator B-24 bombers. He promised to produce one plane every hour.

PEARL HARBOR

Many months before Willow Run was completed, the United States began fighting in World War II. This is how it happened:

For several years, relations between Japan and the United States had worsened. Japan's invasion of China and other Asian countries led the United States to take actions that ended trade between Japan and the United States. The Japanese wanted to push the United States out of Asia. On December 7, 1941, they attacked the United States naval forces that were anchored at Pearl Harbor in Hawaii.

Frank Stock of Hamtramck was at Pearl Harbor on the United States ship *USS Vestal.* Frank remembers that some of the

The Japanese attack on the U.S. naval fleet at Pearl Harbor on December 7, 1941 shocked Americans. The next day, the United States declared war.

sailors were working on the deck. Around 8:00 A.M. they saw airplanes streaking across the harbor. The sailors thought they were U.S. planes.

Suddenly a bomb fell. A sailor saw the red circle on a plane's wing. He shouted, "Those aren't ours! Those are Japanese!"

Two bombs smashed through the deck of Frank's ship. But Frank's commander did not let the men abandon the ship. Instead the ship sailed toward the shore. It ran

In late 1940 these recently drafted Michigan men left Detroit for the Army. World War II had begun and the draft was part of the U.S. effort to be ready for possibly joining that war.

aground on a coral reef. It was damaged, but it did not sink. Later the vessel would be repaired and used in the war.

The next day the United States declared war on Japan. Japan, Germany and Italy had an agreement to help each other in time of war. So on December 11, Germany and Italy declared war on the United States. Soon many Michigan men were among the soldiers fighting in the Pacific and in Europe.

FACTORIES AT WAR

After war was declared, Michigan's factories made even more war supplies.

Michigan had 4 percent of the nation's people, but it produced 10 percent of the nation's war-related goods.

In February 1942 the last wartime passenger car came off the assembly line. From then until the end of the war, the automobile factories would make war supplies instead of cars. In southeast Michigan, Nash made engines and propellors. Hudson build antiaircraft guns. Packard and Studebaker produced airplane engines. Other auto factories made machine guns, airplane parts, torpedoes and ammunition.

Other factories also changed to war production. Kellogg's in Battle Creek made K

The Willow Run Bomber Plant near Ypsilanti had an assembly line over one mile long. During World War II, the plant produced over 8,500 bombers.

Rations—the lightweight emergency food soldiers carried. People at Iron Mountain made gliders. At Kalamazoo they made tanks that could operate on both land and water. Grand Rapids supplied aircraft parts, and Bay City made small warships. Upper Peninsula mines produced copper and iron.

Ford's Willow Run bomber plant was completed by September 1942. Its assembly line was a mile long—the longest in the nation. At first the company did not produce many planes. But by the end of 1943, it was making more than one plane an hour, and by the end of the war, it had produced 8,500 planes.

WARTIME CHANGES

During the war, people did without many things. Silk was needed for parachutes, so it was not used for women's stockings. Food, gasoline and rubber also were needed for the war. So the government said each person could have only so much of each of these. This was called rationing. People received ration coupons to be turned in when they bought gasoline or tires or food.

Some people volunteered to make bandages for the Red Cross. There were paper and metal shortages. Many children collected scrap metal, such as tin cans, and newspapers so they could be recycled.

Americans everywhere celebrated the end of World War II. Here, 500,000 Detroiters gather in Cadillac Square on August 14, 1945, to mark Japan's surrender.

Families planted Victory Gardens so more food would be available for soldiers.

One thing people did not do without was jobs. Wages were good. The Depression was over. In fact, war production resulted in more jobs than workers. Women took many of these jobs. Other jobs went to people who moved to Michigan from other parts of the country.

RACE IS STILL A PROBLEM

During the war there was not enough housing for all the people who moved to the cities to work in the factories. People were too crowded together, especially in Detroit. Blacks in particular had poor housing. Whites who believed in segregation refused to allow blacks to move to white neighborhoods where there was better housing.

In the factories, some white workers did not like working with blacks. They especially did not like it when black workers got promotions and white workers did not.

Blacks knew they worked as well as whites. They knew their young men were fighting and dying in the war. They did not accept the idea that they should be treated like second-class citizens.

Resentment grew on both sides. Summer heat came early in 1943. Temperatures were in the 90s in June. Tempers flared in

Detroit. On Sunday, June 20, some 100,000 people went to Detroit's Belle Isle Park. That evening as this crowd returned home, blacks and whites began to fight. Rumors about the fight spread and more fighting occurred.

All day Monday different fights started. With the situation out of control, the Army was called in.

After the Army restored order, it was learned that thirty-four persons had died. Nine were white and twenty-five were black. Seventeen of the blacks had been shot by police. Detroit's police force then was virtually all white.

After the riot, President R. J. Thomas of the United Auto Workers proposed a program to prevent future clashes. He suggested more parks and recreational facilities, and more and better housing for black families. He also asked for an end to discrimination against black people in employment. Some of Thomas's ideas were adopted and relations between blacks and whites improved.

THE WAR ENDS

The war ended in Europe on May 8, 1945. It ended in the Pacific on August 14, 1945. People everywhere celebrated.

On the night of August 14, half a million people crowded into downtown Detroit, shouting and cheering. A hundred thousand jammed Campau Square in Grand Rapids. In Battle Creek, hundreds of soldiers at Percy Jones Hospital celebrated. Many were on crutches or in wheelchairs. In Lansing thousands overflowed the capitol grounds and surrounding streets.

The fighting was done, but the countries of the world still had to make peace. Michigan's Senator Arthur Vandenberg of Grand Rapids had once wanted to keep the United States from getting involved with the rest of the world.

The war convinced Vandenberg that the United States needed to be involved in world affairs. He believed the United Nations (UN) could help make the peace last a long time. In the UN all the nations of the world would meet and discuss their problems. The UN would try to prevent war. Because of Vandenberg's great support for the idea of a UN, he was asked to help draft its charter.

CONCLUSION

The Great Depression caused much hardship. People decided that the federal and state governments needed to step in and help.

Some workers turned to labor unions to win better wages and working conditions. The success of strikes like the one in Flint made unions more powerful.

World War II ended the Depression. Michigan factories made many things for the war. Many Michigan people worked and gave up things to help win the war.

Jobs created by war production brought people to Michigan. They were often crowded too closely together. One result of this was increased tension between blacks and whites.

This racial tension was one of the problems Michigan people would have to face in the postwar period, which is the subject of the next chapter.

THE NEXT STORY

As this chapter begins, World War II is over. Michigan is building cars and facing old and new challenges. Some challenges are social. They are caused by things like people moving to suburbs, students needing more colleges and minorities demanding equality. Other challenges are economic. Many of these are tied to the automobile industry. Some of the responses to these and other challenges are changes in state government. You and your teachers, family and neighbors probably remember some of the people and events that are in this chapter.

PEOPLE

George Romney was one of Michigan's governors.

Gerald R. Ford was the first person from Michigan to be president of the United States.

Berry Gordy, Jr., began Motown Records in Detroit.

Martin Luther King, Jr., led the national movement for civil rights.

PLACES

The **Straits of Mackinac** could only be crossed by boat until a beautiful bridge was opened in 1957.

Colleges in **Sault Ste. Marie, Grand Rapids, Saginaw, Rochester, Detroit** and **Big Rapids** became part of the state education system between 1950 and 1970.

WORDS

Suburbs are communities built just outside of large central cities.

With **integration,** blacks and whites attend the same schools and live in the same neighborhoods.

Productivity measures how many products a person or a factory can make.

Inflation occurs when prices and wages go up, but the quality and quantity of the things being bought does not.

A **recession** is a time when people buy and make fewer things.

An **income tax** is a tax based on how much a person earns.

Reapportionment is the process of redrawing the boundary lines of voting districts.

The **civil rights movement** was an effort to secure for all people equal rights to do things like vote, go to school and work.

WHEN DID IT HAPPEN?

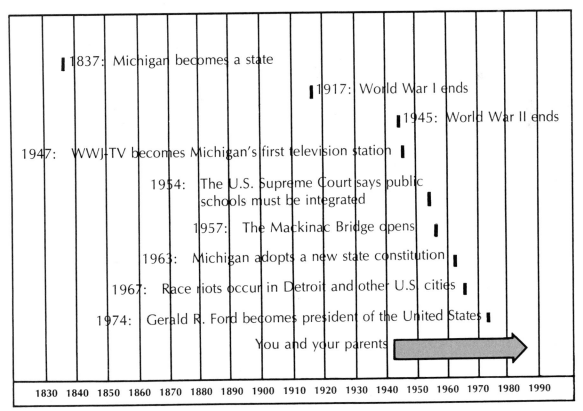

1837: Michigan becomes a state

1917: World War I ends

1945: World War II ends

1947: WWJ-TV becomes Michigan's first television station

1954: The U.S. Supreme Court says public schools must be integrated

1957: The Mackinac Bridge opens

1963: Michigan adopts a new state constitution

1967: Race riots occur in Detroit and other U.S. cities

1974: Gerald R. Ford becomes president of the United States

You and your parents

| 1830 | 1840 | 1850 | 1860 | 1870 | 1880 | 1890 | 1900 | 1910 | 1920 | 1930 | 1940 | 1950 | 1960 | 1970 | 1980 | 1990 |

CHAPTER FIFTEEN MICHIGAN: OUR RECENT PAST

It was Christmas morning 1948. In a house in Royal Oak, a mother, a father and their eight-year-old son and three-year-old daughter were opening their presents. Mom began unwrapping an unusually big box. It stood almost as tall as her eight-year-old son. Finally she got the box open.

"A TV! Joe, a TV!" she cried, hugging her husband. "We wanted that more than anything."

Before 1948 hardly any families had TV. The first Detroit station had begun broadcasting only the year before, in 1947. It was WWJ-TV, now known as WDIV-TV. The first Michigan television station outside Detroit went on the air in Grand Rapids in 1949. It was called WOOD-TV, now WOTV.

The Royal Oak family's new TV only showed pictures in black and white. There was no color TV.

The first programs were mostly "laugh" shows. Their stars were radio and stage comedians such as Milton Berle. Then, on Sunday, November 18, 1951, a brand new show called *See It Now* appeared on TV. It was a serious program starring Edward R. Murrow.

Murrow, wearing a bow tie, told his nationwide audience, "For the first time in the history of man, we are able to look out at both the Atlantic and Pacific coasts of this great country at the same time. . . . No journalistic age was ever given a weapon for truth with quite the scope of this fledgling television."

Other programs, both serious and funny, soon followed. Television began to change the habits of families. No longer did mom and dad and the kids go out so often in the evening to visit neighbors or to see a movie. They did not read as many books or play as many games with each other.

Television was only one of many things that changed the way Michigan people lived between 1945 and the 1980s. Like television, many of the changes affected people throughout the United States and the world. In this chapter, we will focus on some of the events and changes that had the biggest effect on Michigan.

UNIONS GROW STRONGER

Michigan's automobile factories stopped making passenger cars during World War II. So when the war ended, many people wanted new cars. Factories began producing them by the thousands. There was plenty of work in the auto factories, but the workers were not happy.

The union members had not wanted any long strikes during the war because they knew the soldiers could not wait for the supplies they were making. Once the war was over, these workers wanted higher wages. They asked to see the financial records of General Motors (GM) to see if GM could afford to pay them more. GM refused, and on November 21, 1945, the United Auto Workers (UAW) went on strike.

The UAW and GM finally reached an agreement on March 13, 1946. Neither side got everything it wanted, but the union showed that it was strong. Unions would continue to get higher wages and more fringe benefits, such as health insurance, for their members.

Government programs also helped workers. During the Great Depression people had decided that the government should help people who had no jobs. The support of union members helped continue these programs. Under these programs, workmen hurt on the job are paid workman's compensation until they can go back to work. People who lose their jobs are paid unemployment compensation. Employers must contribute money to the programs that make these payments.

THE EDUCATION BOOM

The return of peace and of higher wages meant that people could do things they had put off during the Depression and the war. For many this meant going to college. For others it meant having children. Such a large number of children were born after 1945 that the period is often called "the baby boom."

One result of the baby boom and the number of people going to college was that Michigan public schools and colleges grew rapidly. Between 1950 and 1960 Michigan public school enrollment grew from 1,068,871 students to 1,585,164.

In 1940, Michigan State University had 7,000 students. By 1949, it had 16,000. In 1968, it had 38,758 students. The other state universities grew too, and Ferris State in Big Rapids and Wayne State in Detroit joined the state system. By 1970, four new state colleges had been built. They were Grand Valley State College, Saginaw Valley

Following World War II, Michigan State University grew rapidly. The school's enrollment in 1940 was 7,000, by 1968 it was nearly 40,000.

State College, Lake Superior State College and Oakland University. During this same period (1945-1970), many communities opened two-year colleges.

THE SUBURBS GROW

During the Depression and the war, people also delayed buying homes. After the war, there was a rush to buy houses. Many of the new houses were in the suburbs outside the central city. Churches, stores and businesses moved to the suburbs too. People depended on their cars more and more. Businessmen did special things to attract people with cars. They built drive-in movies, drive-in restaurants, drive-through banks and shopping malls.

The suburbs offered new schools, new stores and healthy surroundings. But they also pulled people, businesses and tax money out of the cities.

With less money, the cities were forced to spend less on schools, police and fire protection, street repair and other services. The cities began to look run down. This made more people want to move to the suburbs. Since the 1950s, people have been trying to find ways to keep the cities from decaying. Kalamazoo did this by turning its downtown area into a mall.

213

Diane Ross and the Supremes (left) and Detroit Mayor Coleman Young (right) are two examples of Michigan's more recent important black celebrities.

Secretary of State Richard Austin (left) is Michigan's highest serving elected black official. John Conyers of Detroit (right) has served in Congress since 1965.

Detroit built new buildings like Cobo Hall along its river front.

INTEGRATION BEGINS

During and after World War II, thousands of blacks moved to Michigan to find better jobs. Detroit's black population went from 149,000 in 1940 to 300,000 in 1950. Across the nation, blacks still faced segregation and discrimination, but things were beginning to change.

Between 1949 and 1951, the U.S. Army ended the segregation of soldiers. In 1954, the U.S. Supreme Court said schools no longer could be segregated.

Some blacks in Michigan were very successful. One was Berry Gordy, Jr. In 1959, Gordy borrowed $700 to start a recording company. He called it Motown Records. Motown recording artists included Diana Ross and the Supremes. The Motown sound soon made Gordy a top seller of popular records.

In civic affairs, Otis M. Smith of Flint was among the black leaders in Michigan government. He was Michigan's auditor general and a member of the Michigan Supreme Court.

In spite of changes and successes like these, most blacks lived in the oldest, most crowded and rundown neighborhoods in the cities. Most had low-paying jobs. They had little influence on government. They often faced discrimination. For example, restaurants might refuse to serve them because they were black.

Many black people believed that the best way to fight discrimination was to hold peaceful rallies and try to change laws.

Their leader was Dr. Martin Luther King, Jr. On June 23, 1963, King came to Detroit. About 125,000 white and black people marched with him down Woodward Avenue to the river front. There King used the words that would become famous in the August 1963 civil rights march in Washington, D.C.—"I have a dream." His dream was of blacks and whites "walking together hand in hand, free at last."

Other blacks believed violence was needed if change was to come fast enough. In the mid-1960s blacks and whites were involved in riots in cities in the United States. Michigan's riots came in 1967.

THE 1967 RIOTS

In the summer of 1967, many blacks were angry because integration was not happening fast enough. They were frustrated because so many blacks could not find jobs. They thought more blacks should be on the Detroit police force. They resented the fact that white people owned most of the stores and apartments in black neighborhoods.

On June 23, Detroit policemen raided a bar that was serving liquor illegally. The bar was in a black neighborhood. The police began to arrest people. A crowd gathered. People in the crowd got angry. They began to break store windows. Soon the crowd was out of control. A riot had begun.

It took a week to stop the Detroit riot. There were smaller riots in other Michigan cities. The riots shocked Michigan. The state legislature and local governments strengthened police forces. They also tried to stop discrimination against

The Detroit riot of July 1967 left 43 people dead, 1,700 stores looted, 1,400 buildings burned and property damage amounting to $50 million. Above is one burned-out city block.

blacks. For example, in 1968, the state made it illegal to refuse to rent or sell a home to a person because of that person's race.

Blacks began to play a more important role in Michigan politics. In 1974, for example, Coleman Young became Detroit's first black mayor.

Today, people still are working to see that all people have an equal chance to succeed. Their efforts involve Indians, whose ancestors were the first people to live in Michigan. They involve the Chicanos, whose families began coming to Michigan to harvest sugar beets in the early twentieth century. They involve new immigrants and people with handicaps.

THE ECONOMY AND THE CAR

In the 1950s, cars got bigger and fancier. Each year's models looked different. This encouraged people to buy new cars even though their old ones were running well. Car sales boomed. There were problems in the background, but few people worried about them.

One problem was that auto factories were moving from Michigan to other states to be closer to major markets. Another was that machines were replacing factory workers. Both of these problems meant fewer jobs for Michigan workers.

A third problem involved international events. Between 1950 and 1953 the United

216

Michigan automakers responded to the challenge of less expensive imported cars by using robots on the assembly line and making smaller, more efficient automobiles.

States was involved in a war in Korea. Michigan again made arms and military supplies. Workers again came to Michigan. When the war ended, these workers had trouble finding other jobs. In 1953, some 503,000 people were employed in Michigan auto plants. By 1958, that number had dropped to 293,000.

In the 1970s an even greater problem appeared. It was called inflation. During inflation, prices rise while the quantity of products stays the same. Gasoline that cost 30 cents a gallon in the 1960s cost over one dollar a gallon in the late 1970s. The price of cars rose too. Fewer people could afford big, new cars.

There was now a car market for small, less-expensive cars that went farther on a gallon of gas. Most of the first factories to make cars for this new market were in other countries, such as Japan and Germany. As sales of U.S. cars dropped, Michigan was hurt more than most states. One firm, Chrysler, got a loan from the U.S. government so that it would not have to close its doors. The labor unions cooperated by agreeing not to demand pay raises. This helped keep the price of cars from going even higher.

Michigan also worked hard to strengthen other parts of its economy and to find new kinds of industry and business.

Completed in 1957, the Mackinac Bridge links Michigan's peninsulas at the Straits of Mackinac. Over five miles in length, it is the world's longest suspension bridge.

AGRICULTURE

Michigan farmers grow over 50 different food crops. Only California produces more kinds of crops. In the early 1980s Michigan led the nation in producing blueberries, sour cherries, pickling cucumbers, navy beans and eastern soft white winter wheat. It ranked among the nation's 5 leaders in 17 other agricultural products.

One tragic accident hurt Michigan agriculture in the 1970s. A manufacturing company accidentally mixed a fire retardant chemical called PBB with livestock feed. The feed was eaten by livestock. Many cattle died or had to be killed. Eventually traces of PBB were found in food and humans. The accident led to tighter control of the use of chemicals.

Agriculture makes money for Michigan in two ways. First, farmers sell crops like wheat or cherries. Second, food processors prepare those crops for market by making such products as cereal or canned fruit. One way to strengthen agriculture is to have more food processing done in Michigan.

Michigan offers tourists 11,000 lakes and miles of Great Lakes coastline.

TOURISM

Tourism is another large part of Michigan's economy. One reason Michigan excels in tourism is its parks, forests, lakes and streams. It had 92 state parks and recreation areas in the early 1980s, plus 3 national parks. It has more acres of state-owned forest than any other state. Michigan also offers tourists exciting cities and the Great Lakes.

Mackinac Island was the state's first tourist attraction. As early as 1838 people went to Mackinac Island for vacations. In 1887 investors built the Grand Hotel there. The railroads built other large tourist hotels in Petoskey, Harbor Springs and Charlevoix. People came for northern Michigan's cool summers and beautiful scenery. After World War II, Michigan began building ski resorts and became a year-round tourist state.

Michigan's good highway system also attracts tourists. Part of that system is the Mackinac Bridge, which connects Michigan's upper and lower peninsulas. Before it opened, people had to take ferry boats to get from one peninsula to the other.

People had talked about a bridge since 1884. But it had to be very long to cross the Straits of Mackinac. It also had to be strong because of the high winds that blow across the straits. It took four years to build the bridge, which was completed in 1957.

The bridge is a pathway to such Upper Peninsula attractions as the Tahquamenon Falls, the ship locks at Sault Ste. Marie, Historic Fayette Townsite, Fort Wilkins and Pictured Rocks National Lakeshore.

GOVERNMENT CHANGES

As Michigan's society and economy changed, its government had to change too. One change was in the power held by the rural and urban parts of the state. Others were in the way the government was organized and in the way it raised money.

The legislators who make Michigan's laws each represent a geographic district of the state. In the 1950s more and more people moved to the cities and their suburbs, but the legislative district boundaries did not change. Because of this, people

219

from rural areas had more political power than those from urban areas. In 1960 one Upper Peninsula senator represented 55,000 people. At the same time, the senator from Oakland County represented 690,000 people.

A second problem in the 1950s was the financing of state government. Michigan was running programs for workers who were hurt on the job or unemployed. It was building colleges. It was helping cities. These programs cost money.

Government gets most of its money from taxes. There was not enough tax money to pay Michigan's bills.

In 1959, the state borrowed $95 million to help pay for programs. But when payday came on May 5, the state did not have enough money to pay the people who worked for it. The state employees had to wait until the next week to get paid.

People across the state decided some changes needed to be made. One person, George Romney, started a group called Citizens for Michigan. In 1961 Romney convinced Democrats and Republicans that Michigan should hold a convention to write a new constitution. He hoped the constitution would deal with the unequal legislative districts and state finances.

In 1962, Romney was elected governor of Michigan. And in 1963, voters approved the constitution that had been written at the convention.

THE NEW CONSTITUTION

The constitution said that the boundaries of the voting districts in Michigan would be redrawn every 10 years. This change,

William G. Milliken of Traverse City was governor of Michigan for 14 years.

called reapportionment, would give people living in urban areas more power.

The constitution made state government less complex and more efficient. It combined 130 state agencies, bureaus and commissions into no more than 20 departments. One of the departments was a civil rights commission to help stop racial discrimination in Michigan.

The constitution also said the governor would be elected for four instead of two years. The governor is elected in a year that is not an election year for the U.S. president. This was done so that people would think about state instead of national issues when they elected their governor.

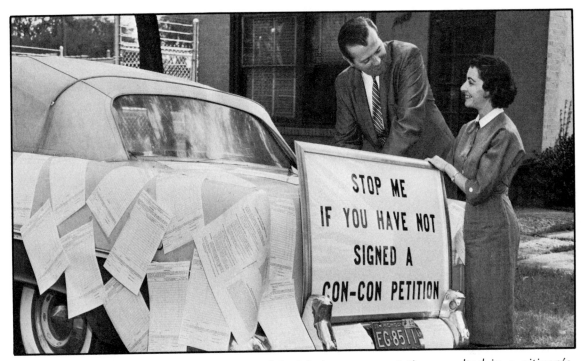

The need to improve state financing and legislative representation resulted in a citizen's petition drive to call a state constitutional convention in 1961.

Turning to finances, the new constitution said that Michigan must have a balanced budget. This meant the state could not spend more money than it took in. The constitution also allowed the state to tax the income that people earned. However, an income tax was not adopted until 1967.

CONCLUSION

The constitution did not solve all of Michigan's problems. Many people in the state are still concerned that taxes and government spending are too high. Others want the government to do more for education or other special programs. The constitution did show that when Michigan

people work together, they can make changes and try new things.

Many of the challenges discussed in this chapter continue. Labor unions still go on strike when they think management is unfair. State leaders continue to encourage businesses to come to and stay in Michigan. Central cities still struggle to survive. But Michigan has overcome challenges and problems before. When Michigan ran out of furs and timber, many people thought it would become a poor state. But as Governor John Swainson once noted, "We met those challenges and we are going to meet future challenges because our people are well trained, energetic and very skillful."

PICTURE CREDITS

Many of the illustrations appearing in *People of Forest and City* can be found in the vast photographic collections of the Michigan State Archives in Lansing. The editors wish to thank Photo Archivist John Curry for his assistance in selecting these illustrations. Illustrations not from the State Archives are listed below following the page where they appear.

Page 6, 7: John Halsey; 11 (bottom), 26, 27, 38 (top), 45 (right), 55, 77, 86 (bottom): Robert Thom paintings; 4-5, 12 (left), 18-19, 23 (bottom), 42-43, 60-61, 69 (left), 74-75, 81, 83, 92-93, 110-11, 126-27: Susan Price; 12 (top and bottom right): Frances Densmore's *Chippewa Customs*, Bureau of American Ethnology; 14,15: Harbor Springs Historical Commission; 29: William L. Clements Library; 32-33, 142-43, 156-57, 168-69, 182-83, 196-97, 210-11: Kelly Nelson; 46, 47, 56: Mackinac Island State Park Commission; 50 (top): Chicago Historical Society; 53 (top left): Toronto Public Library; 64 (bottom): Eerdman's Publishing Company; 66 (top): Lee Benson; 94: *Michigan Pioneer and Historical Collection;* 96 (top left), 191: Ben Wilson, Western Michigan University; 96 (top right): *Lisette* by Isabella E. Swan; 102: *Hastings Banner;* 104: Detroit Institute of Art; 114: Western Michigan University Regional Archives and Historical Collections; 123: *The West Point Atlas of American Wars*, Volume One, compiled by the Department of Military Art and Engineering, West Point, NY; 136, 137: Gerald Micketti; 162: Michigan State University Archives and Historical Collections; 174: Henry Ford Archives; 213: Michigan State University; 215 (top right): City of Detroit; 215 (bottom right): Congressman John Conyers; 217: Oldsmobile Corporation; 219: Travel Bureau, Michigan Department of Commerce.

INDEX